Who Killed Betsy?

Uncovering Penn State University's Most Notorious
Unsolved Crime

By Derek Sherwood

Cover Design: Heather Meadows Design

Front Cover: Betsy Aardsma and Pattee Library.
Back Cover : Richard Haefner on a geology trip, 1967.

Published by Pine Grove Press, LLC.
2nd printing

LCCN: 2011933764
ISBN 13: 9780615498119

"If you keep digging long enough and have enough patience, something will come out."

–Unsigned note in the Penn State Special Collections Betsy Aardsma file, attributed to William Kimmel.

Table of Contents

Introduction

There is something profoundly unsettling about an unsolved murder. We have created a world where our police officers inspire faith in their ability to protect us from crime and criminals, and we watch television shows where every cold case is neatly wrapped up within forty-eight minutes, not counting commercials. In real life, however, things are often not as simple. Witnesses fail to come forward; politics prevent a complete investigation; and in some cases, the evidence just isn't there.

Unsolved murder is even more unsettling when the victim is someone like us. A college student, working on a class project in the library, is murdered over Thanksgiving break. Witnesses see the probable killer leave the building, and still no one is caught. These murders are perhaps the most disturbing. What's even more disturbing is that the scenario just described actually happened in the Pattee Library at Pennsylvania State University on November 28th, 1969, to English graduate student Elizabeth Ruth Aardsma.

There have been three unsolved murders in Penn State in the last century – the brutal killing of Penn State student Rachel Taylor in the 1941, then the murder of Betsy Aardsma in 1969, and finally the savage stabbing death of Dana Bailey in her off-campus apartment in 1987. All were horrifying – all changed the lives of everyone involved. Only one was committed on University property, however, and that one murder has captured the thoughts of nearly everyone who has heard the rumors of it.

The Betsy Aardsma murder is conveniently inconvenient for Penn State. They have done little to come clean about the crime. Campus tour guides will often speak of "a girl being murdered in the library," but they're not supposed to – and when pressed, they will tell you "We're not really allowed to talk about that." The Aardsma murder adds to the legends of the campus – haunted dorms, mysterious testing done in the water tunnel -- but at the same time, it is a black spot on the University's history and reputation, There are reasons for this, perhaps – but hindsight is 20/20, and perhaps the University did everything they could to help prevent the crime, or at least solve it once it had happened. Whatever the case, the crime was never solved.

At times, investigating an unsolved murder case is much like the work of an archaeologist or paleontologist – care must be taken that once the dust of history has been disturbed, no damage is done to the potentially priceless artifacts that are being uncovered. In many cases, individuals who have knowledge in cases like this will only talk once or twice, and then will stop telling their story – which makes it extremely important that the story is taken completely the first time. Once someone has decided they are not going to talk about a murder case, they rarely change their mind.

Other aspects of investigating a cold case require classic collegiate research skills – slogging through old reels of microfiche; researching among dusty newspapers and other traditional primary sources. These can only tell you so much, though, and then you must rely on the skills of a salesman – the willingness to cold call strangers and attempt to talk to them about unpleasant events, or to drop by and take someone you've never met out to lunch while simultaneously trying to get them to tell you what they know about your subject.

The Internet has changed the face of historical research forever, and in many good ways. One such way is in the availability of primary sources online, as well as the ease by which you can find someone without the use of the phone book or directory assistance. Legal cases are much more available now that many courthouses are digitizing their records, and if not, it is easy enough to request to have copies sent to you.

This book is the culmination of three years of research into the Aardsma murder, and would not have been possible without the help of a number of individuals, including Sascha Skucek, who has worked on the Aardsma case since 1999, and Pamela West, who investigated the case in the 1980s. Each of us has tried in our own way to bring some closure to the case, using vastly different methods and means. All of this effort has been dedicated to one end: solving the mystery of "Who killed Betsy?"

So Damned Squeaky Clean

In newspaper articles and interviews with former classmates and friends, Betsy Aardsma has been described as "one step shy of a saint," and while that description accurately covers the cleanliness of her personal life relative to why she might have been a target for murder, it does her a disservice in other areas. Betsy Ruth Aardsma was much like any college student of the 1960s, especially a female college student, coming up in a world where women's rights, the Vietnam War, and Civil Rights were on the tip of everyone's tongue. To really understand who Betsy Aardsma was, you first have to understand the environment from which she came: Holland, Michigan.

Holland Michigan is a conservative town on the shores of Lake Michigan, roughly parallel with Milwaukee across the Great Lakes. Holland, which calls itself the "All American City with a Dutch Accent," continues many of the traditions of the Old World and the Netherlands, where many of its families originate from. Tulip Festivals, Dutch colonial architecture, and museums focused on Dutch heritage and culture are

7

spread out throughout the thriving town. Dutch names –
like Aardsma – are common, and many of the families
here can trace their own heritage back to the great
families of the Netherlands.

It was into this environment that Elizabeth Ruth
"Betsy" Aardsma was born on July 11th, 1947, to Richard
and Esther Aardsma. Betsy's father worked as a sales
tax auditor for the Michigan state government, while
Esther stayed home to raise the four children. The
family was close knit and religious, regularly attending
the Trinity Reformed Church of Holland, Michigan.
Betsy's sister Carole would later go on to become a
minister.

After graduation from Holland High School, where
she placed fifth in her class, Betsy decided to become
involved in outreach efforts run by her church. These led
to her spending time at a Navajo Indian reservation in
the southwestern United States, as well as to spending
time teaching art to inner-city students in Grand Rapids,
Michigan. Unsure of whether she wanted to pursue a
career in medicine or some other field, Betsy entered
Hope College in the fall of 1965, where she majored in
pre-medicine. She had originally wanted to attend the
University of Michigan at Ann Arbor for her

undergraduate work, but pressure from her parents convinced her to stay at Hope, which had a strong pre-med program and would provide her with a great start to her higher education.

At 5'8" tall, with a slim figure, long reddish brown hair and hazel eyes, Betsy cut a dramatic and fetching image. While never knockout beauty, she was considered attractive and had no problem attracting the interests of men in her life. She was more interested in her studies and her future, however, and for the most part, her dating experiences were casual and friendly, but not serious.

Betsy dated a number of young men at Hope College, but didn't seem to find any serious boyfriend material while she was there. She had a few short-lived relationships with men, who found her attractive, but she never seemed to connect with any of them on a deeper level. For the most part, these relationships, while short-lived, were friendly, although at some point Betsy was threatened by a former boyfriend, a story that involves her having a knife pulled on her, or the threat of having a knife pulled on her. She was terrified by the ordeal, but it apparently wasn't that serious, and didn't result in any charges.

Her friends recall a young woman who was somewhat feminist and intent on the idea that she would become a doctor. She was a girl who liked to sneak cigarettes with her friends, as well as to write in her journals, spend time with her girlfriends, and pay attention to the changes going on in the world around her. By her sophomore year at Hope College, Betsy had decided that she would transfer to the University of Michigan at Ann Arbor.

Betsy arrived at the University of Michigan in time for the Fall 1967 semester, where the war against Vietnam was in full swing. The campus, which had seen the inception of the radical organization Students for a Democratic Society, was at that time host to Bill Ayers, who would go on to garner notice as a leader of SDS in 1968 and 1969 before helping to form a splinter group known as the Weathermen that advocated militancy over peaceful protest and would go on to plant bombs and kill people in the pursuit of their goals. Betsy, although a later supporter of McCarthy and his opposition to Johnson in 1968, managed to stay out of the whirlwind of protests that surrounded her at the University of Michigan.

It was during her senior year in 1968-69 that she met the man who would become her steady boyfriend. David Wright, a fraternity brother living with some friends in an apartment above the one Betsy rented in her senior year, would become Betsy's steady boyfriend, as well as the driving force behind her transfer to Penn State. Wright, the good-looking pre-med student from Illinois who had captured Betsy's heart, had decided to go to Penn State Hershey Medical School to get his medical degree. The two had been dating for some time when he told her of his interest in attending Penn State. It was clear that she had a decision to make.

Betsy had transferred to the English department when she attended University of Michigan, having given up on her pre-med desires in favor of the literature and poetry that she loved. She was interested in helping others, as evidenced by her work at the Navajo reservation, and she was fascinated by Africa, and the plight of the people there. Betsy had made up her mind that she was going to join the Peace Corps, and spend time in Africa, helping to improve the living situation on the continent. David told her that he couldn't guarantee that he would wait for her if she joined the Peace Corps, and she reluctantly decided to pursue graduate studies

11

at Penn State main campus while he attended Penn State Hershey.

It was a propitious decision on her part. Betsy was aware of the serial killings that had been taking place in Ann Arbor since March of 1969. A serial killer was on the loose, and he was targeting young, attractive co-eds. Betsy was as excited to leave Ann Arbor as she was disappointed to be leaving her friends behind – she had graduated with "honors and distinction" in English that spring – but by all accounts she was looking forward to the graduate program at Penn State, and to spending time with her boyfriend David.

Once she arrived at Penn State, Betsy spent most of her time studying. She had little interest in outside activities, and the English graduate program was aggressive and tough. At times, she wondered what she was doing there, and whether or not she should drop out of the program. Her friends and roommates recall that she wrote frequently to her boyfriend David, even doing so the day she died – her last letter arrived to him on the Saturday following her murder. Weekends were spent traveling down to Hershey to spend time with David and his roommates. Most of her friends at Ann Arbor and Penn State did not realize how dedicated she was to

David, as she tended to keep her feelings to herself, and did not gush about her boyfriend.

After she died, the rumor would come out that they were engaged, but David Wright said that wasn't the case "Everyone says we were engaged -- we were not engaged," David said. "We were looking at rings, the idea was that we would be engaged by Christmas. But no, I hadn't given her a ring at that point." Betsy's first goal was to finish her education and become a college professor or teacher. Happy to be out of Ann Arbor, Betsy was still introspective about her life and her future. She often asked her friends hypothetically about whether or not she wanted to be a doctor's wife: "Do I want the house with the white picket fence and the keys to the Country Squire?"

While she may have doubted the path her life was taking, she remained devoted to David, and even a little bit jealous. Once, a female friend of David's who had broken up with her boyfriend came over to seek advice from David. He and the girl spent the evening playing cards at his apartment, innocently taking her mind off of her personal problems. When Betsy found out, she was furious, and apparently an argument ensued. Other than that, the two were fairly close and virtually inseparable.

The biggest wrong assumption that was made in the Aardsma murder case came from the fact that the police never seriously considered that a jilted former suitor could potentially have been responsible for her murder. The concepts of murderous stalkers and vengeful lovers were not new in 1969, but there was not as much focus on it as there has been in the modern era. Either out of an attempt to keep Aardsma's public memory clean, or out of a simple act of overlooking the facts, the police never let on that Betsy had been on several dates with other individuals since she had transferred to Penn State.

At one time or another, several of her English 501 classmates took her out for coffee and conversation. These do not seem to have been serious dates. The media either never found out about, or chose not to mention these dates, which police became aware of as their investigation progressed. This is not to say that she had done anything wrong or unfaithful to Wright by exploring her options or deciding to test the waters of Penn State to see if there was someone else out there for her; it merely serves to show that Betsy was not as

14

secure in her relationship as others seemed to think. As usual, Betsy kept her feelings to herself, and did not write about these men in her diary or talk about her relationship doubts to her friends or roommate Sharon Brandt.

Outside of her social life, Penn State was a whirlwind of activity similar to the University of Michigan campus at Ann Arbor. Rising racial tensions had produced a number of protests by black students, who argued that the school was not keeping with the times in bringing up black enrollment as well as increasing the number of African-American professors at the school. At one point on 1968, demonstrators had taken over the Old Main building to protest the assassination of Martin Luther King, Jr., holding a number of faculty and administration members hostage for nearly half a day and releasing a list of demands to the press. All was not well in Happy Valley, but the college environment there was still quaint and somewhat behind the times. Things move at a slower pace in State College.

It has been written that Betsy became more active in anti-war demonstrations during her eight short weeks at Penn State, but this is not entirely correct. An article in the Harrisburg Patriot News in December 2008 stated that Betsy had led a campus discussion group against the war during the National Moratorium Day on October 15th, 1969. Some suggested that perhaps she had angered someone by doing so, resulting in her murder. This was a reportorial error, however. The October 15th Moratorium Day involved a former Pennsylvania gubernatorial candidate, Milton Schapp, addressing 1700 students at the Schwab Auditorium, where he urged an end to hostilities in Vietnam. That night, after the protests, 4,000 students marched across campus to the Garfield Thomas Water Tunnel, an underground testing site for classified military technologies such as submarine armaments and other equipment.

Betsy was involved in leading only one anti-war discussion that is on record – a workshop held during Moratorium Week in November. Moratorium Week is a deceptive term, as the November Moratorium activities lasted only four days, from 11/13-11/17/69. On 11/13/69, a series of hour-long workshops were held in the HUB Student Union Building -- 6-7 workshops per hour, with a total of 30-40 workshops that day. Betsy's workshop, entitled "The War and Black Authors," held in HUB 215 at 12:30 PM that afternoon, was surely among the tamest and ostensibly least offensive of the topics, some of which bore titles like "The Power Elite and the War," "US Foreign Policy and Revolution," and "Imperialism: The Highest State of Capitalism."

Aside from her single Vietnam War protest experience, Betsy spent most of her time working on her English 501 research. By Thanksgiving, 1969, she was feeling stressed and had fallen behind on her research. After spending Thanksgiving with her boyfriend David Wright and his roommates and their girlfriends, Betsy made the fateful and impromptu decision to return to Penn State the following day to meet with her professors and get a jump on the research paper she needed to write to complete the class. The last time Wright would ever see her was when he drove her to the bus station on Thanksgiving night so that she could return to Penn State that evening. Roommate Sharon Brandt recalled that they stayed up that night playing cards and talking for a few hours before turning in for the evening.

Police would later search her diaries for any evidence of problems with other students or concerns, but they could find none. The closest Betsy came to possibly trying to reach out to anyone regarding her uneasy feelings at Penn State came when she started telling David Wright that she had considered transferring to Penn State Harrisburg to be closer to him, roughly in late October, 1969. Wright would later recall that, "In retrospect, when I thought about that, I wondered if she was worried about something up there. My wife's theory is that she just wanted to move things along and be closer."

Investigator Ron Tyger, both at the time and even years later, made the statement that she was "so damned squeaky clean it was pathetic," and that unlike most college students of the era, "there was nothing in her room that you wouldn't be ashamed to tell her parents about."

In addition to the image of Betsy Aardsma that came out as a free-spirited, intelligent young woman, interested in the world around her and unsure of her position in it, police would make two interesting statements in news articles that came out after her murder. They stated that they felt that Aardsma may have known her killer, since she had been approached from the front and had not screamed or otherwise attempted to flee. They also stated that, after extensive research, they felt that she had not been followed or otherwise targeted.

18

According to the police, no one expected her to be at Penn State that day, and no one could have predicted her meandering path from her dorm to the Burrowes building to meet with Joukovsky and then to the library. These statements quickly became buried in the information released to the media surrounding the case, but they are vital to understanding her death.

If Betsy had not been scheduled to be at Penn State that day, the killer must also have been at Penn State, possibly sharing a dorm room that would have given him the ability to notice her comings and goings. He may have seen her leave with her roommate that day, and he may have anticipated where she was going. If the killer lived in the same dorm as she did, he could also have followed her without appearing out of place – he was just another student going about his business. If he knew her, he could have stalked her or anticipated where he might find her without ever raising any flags to her roommates or friends.

Twenty Minutes in the Core

The last hours of Betsy Aardsma's life started innocently enough when she left her dorm room in the afternoon of November 28th, 1969 with her roommate, Sharon Brandt. The pair headed towards Pattee Library, where they split up; agreeing to meet later for either dinner or a movie, with "Easy Rider" and "Take the Money and Run" both on the table as potential cinematic entertainment for the evening. Betsy headed to meet with Harrison Meserole and Nicholas Joukovsky, her professors in English 501. Betsy met with Joukovsky first, around 4:00 PM, promising to visit the Pattee stacks after she met with Meserole to bring back a book she had used as a source in a previous project that Joukovsky was interested in. Then she headed for her meeting with Meserole in his office on Level 1 of Pattee Library.

On her way into the library, Betsy ran into her classmates and friends Linda Marsa and Rob Steinberg, who later told police that they had seen her entering through the front doors of the library as they were leaving. This fact would prove crucial to establishing the timeline of Betsy Aardsma's last hour, as sightings by friends would help PA State Police investigators to piece together the specifics of her movements during the time period between 4:00 and 5:00 PM. After chatting with them briefly, Betsy continued on her way down to see Meserole.

Harrison Meserole, or "Harry" as he was known to friends, was an interesting and imposing character – the eight hundred pound gorilla in the room that was the PSU English department in the 1960s. A sizeable man, weighing over three hundred pounds -- who appeared to one colleague as a "clean-shaven Santa," and who walked with a distinctive shuffle due to a brace he wore on his legs to assist with his diabetes -- Meserole had an ego as large as his bulky frame. In later years, the diabetes caused him to lose a great deal of weight, but in 1969 he was at his peak mass, both physically and metaphorically, and his place in the hierarchy of Penn State's English department was unquestioned.

By 1969, Meserole had done what was considered to be virtually impossible in the academic world – he had successfully transitioned from his original role as assistant professor at Penn State where he was appointed in 1960, to full professor, which he was appointed to in 1965. One of his later colleagues called this feat "the academic equivalent of running a sub-four-minute mile." It was well known among his students that Meserole had the power to make or break an English grad student within the first semester or two, and currying favor and staying on his good side was the only way to survive the program.

Already a lion of the PSU English Department at the age of 48, Meserole had a biting wit and a penchant for smoking in class. He and Joukovsky co-taught the English 501 class, with Joukovsky's focus being on English and European literature, and Meserole's interests and instruction being focused on Early American literature. He spent a great deal of time working with the World Shakespeare Bibliography in the later 1970s, when he was not delving into such topics as seventeenth century American poets, or helping to create the precursor to the *MLA Handbook*, essentially the foremost work on the MLA Style.

Besides his work as an English professor, Meserole was in charge of handling the biographical portions of the PMLA, the journal of the Modern Language Association, throughout most of the years between 1957 and 1975. His office, located in the basement of Pattee, was conveniently located near the men's room, and near the offices where his army of student volunteers were hard at work diligently typing and transcribing the MLA work he assigned to them. Assisting him in his office as an assistant and paid contributor to the MLA work that he did was his twenty-something secretary Patricia Letterman, many years his junior, who lived with him in a strange ménage-et-trois arrangement at his house along with his wife. Years later, after the death of his first wife, Patricia would become his second wife, almost as if by default.

Meserole's schedule was packed with appointments that day, and he and Patricia had some recollection of Betsy's visit. Meserole found Betsy to be "beautiful" and captivating, and Patricia recalled that Betsy had been on time for her appointment, but that the student scheduled to meet with them after Betsy left had cancelled. This left Meserole with some free time, which he may have used to look at one of the many hardcore pornographic magazines he kept in his office, wrapped in brown paper – magazines that he delighted in showing to unsuspecting coeds, usually leading to an embarrassed silence on the part of the unlucky young woman who was receiving the picture show.

It's unknown whether Meserole chose to show Betsy any of his "collection," but if he did, she likely just blushed and said nothing. Meserole's temper and sarcasm were devastating, and no one dared challenge his whims, least of all one of his female students. After a brief respite between his meetings with first semester English 501 students, Meserole's next appointment arrived.

After leaving Meserole's office, Betsy returned to Level 3 and to her graduate study carrel, where she deposited her white jacket, her purse, and a book about Africa, before heading to the card catalog inside the main doors of Pattee, where the "Nittany Lion" now stands encased behind glass. Aardsma was observed inside the library by fellow student Marilee Erdley around 4:30 p.m, when Erdley literally bumped into her near the card catalog. After she found the reference she was seeking, she went back down the narrow stairs into the Level 2 Core, presumably to find the book that she had promised to Joukovsky and that she had just referenced at the card catalog.

Exactly what book she was looking for remains a point of contention to this day. Nicholas Joukovsky taught the European literature side of the class, so it is

24

likely that if Aardsma was looking for a book for a project she had done for him, she would be in a section related to European literature. She was, however, also working on a project for Meserole, who taught the Early American portion of the class, but it makes little sense that she was in Level 2 Core at all that evening.

Dr. Joukovsky has suggested that she had worked on a project for him regarding a parody of a 1665 poem by Edmund Waller that was entitled "Instructions to a Painter." The parody, part of a series with titles such as "The Last Instructions to a Painter" by Andrew Marvell, would have fit well with her Dutch heritage, as the poems describe the Dutch fleet attacking the English Fleet in the Thames River. This is the most complete guess as to what Aardsma may have been searching for, and even Joukovsky is unsure of the title of the book he had asked her to return with that day, or what she was working on for Meserole. In a recent interview, he suggested that the book was "The Life and Works of John Arbuthnot" by G.A. Aiken. Whatever her reason for being there, she had made the fateful decision to head into the Core stacks at Pattee Library that day, an area of the Pattee Library that had just recently been opened to student traffic.

To understand the design and layout of the Pattee Core stacks, it is important to understand that the stacks were never intended to be accessed by students. Originally, Pattee was a "closed stacks" library – meaning that there was a desk in front of the low-slung entrance to the stacks where a student employee would sit during library hours. Anyone wanting to check out a book that was in the stacks would give the student employee the call number of the book, and the employee would enter the stacks to retrieve it while the student waited outside. This was a prevailing theory in many University library designs of the time, partly because it ensured that shrinkage of the book collection due to theft remained low, and partly because it also ensured that books were in their intended places, since students could not idly move them around while browsing or researching.

Moving around inside the stacks is a cramped, claustrophobic experience. The dim fluorescent lights hang at head level, and the aisles and stairs are only about as wide as a single person. The stacks had only been opened to students a year or so prior to the Aardsma murder, and the dark brown vinyl-asbestos tile of the floors and the few timer-operated banks of

26

fluorescent lights offered very little visibility and comfort. The University had thrown a few study carrels into the Stacks area, taken away the desks at the entrances, and called it an open stack library.

The other important fact to understand about the stacks is that, in order to fit more books into the space, each level of the stacks is one half of a normal story or floor. So, the basement, or Level 1 Stacks, and the second floor, or Level 3 Stacks, provide the only points of entrance or egress to the Level 2 Stacks. Level 1 had stairs directly up to Level 3, and Level 3 exited across the lobby and out the front door, but access to Level 2 Core was limited to a small service elevator and a pair of staircases, one on the East side and one on the West side of the core, prior to entering the Eastern or Western stacks proper. There is no direct way out of Level 2 Core besides these two small staircases and the service elevator.

At some point after Aardsma was seen at the card catalog around 4:30, Assistant Stacks Supervisor Dean Brungart strolled through the core, making his rounds before his shift ended at five that day. He later claimed to have seen a girl in a red dress in one aisle alone, with two men talking quietly and among themselves a few aisles over. This likely means that Brungart passed through the core prior to 4:45 PM, which would have given one or both of these men time to leave the core prior to Betsy's murder.

At around 4:45 PM, classmate Shirley Brooks[1] walked down into the Level 2 Core to borrow a pen from Betsy. As she descended the narrow steps, a tanned, mustache-wearing man sporting a brown overcoat passed her coming up the stairs and bumped into her, possibly blurting an apology. When she arrived on Level 2, Brooks found Betsy in one of the center aisles. According to Brooks, the two were alone in the Core, surrounded by volumes of books on England, Germany, and Europe. Brooks asked Betsy to borrow a pen, which she took back to her desk, used, and then returned to Betsy a few minutes later.

While the two may have been alone in the Core, they were not alone in the stacks. In the Eastern portion of the stacks, Joao Uafinda, a geography student from Mozambique, was working on some research, while Marilee Erdley, one of Aardsma's classmates, read at a desk just outside the entrance to the Core stacks, a scant fifteen to twenty feet from Aardsma. Another

---

[1]   Name has been changed.

28

student in the Eastern stacks snored slightly as he slept at one of the drab green study carrels located there.

In the West wing of the stacks, a man named Richard Allen -- a well-renowned aerospace historian from New York -- used a copy machine there while he waited for his son, who he had come to take home for the Thanksgiving weekend.

Allen would later claim when interviewed by the police that he heard a conversation between a man and a woman that was taking place while he used the copy machine. He said that there was nothing unusual or out of the ordinary about the conversation, and that it seemed to be a "normal conversation" between two people. It is likely that Allen overheard a conversation between Betsy and her killer, as only a few moments passed after the conversation took place before a much more unusual sound echoed through the core – a metallic crashing noise.

After the crash, Richard Allen began to move towards the Core when a man came "barreling" out towards him. Allen recalled that the man "looked like a student," and swerved to avoid him, running in a northeasterly direction around the core and towards the Eastern stacks.

29

Allen's son Robert would later recall his father discussing what he had seen: Despite what he had seen, "When dad came back that night, he told me that there had been some kind of commotion in the library. He didn't think anything else of it. None of us did, until a couple of days later -- we heard on the radio that they were looking for witnesses, and I told him 'Dad, you'd better go and talk to them.' They interviewed him once the following week, and I think I recall him coming back from New York once in the spring to be interviewed again. After that, we never heard anything more."

* * *

Newspaper reports described a scream and a crash, along with the sound of books falling – but Erdley and others in the core that day would recall that there was no scream – if anything, a slight gasp, followed by the crashing of books and metal.

Upstairs, in his office on Level 3, Dean Brungart heard the crashing sounds through a ventilation grate in the floor, but he didn't think much of it – it was not unusual for the unwieldy metal carts used by library employees to transport books through the core for shelving to overturn, and besides, it was 5:00 – quitting time.

Meanwhile, after the crash, standing on the East side of the core, Erdley and Uafinda looked at each other, and a moment later a man came rushing out from the direction of the crash.

"That girl needs help," the man said to Erdley. He pointed with his left hand towards the direction of the Core, keeping his right hand concealed at his side. Erdley would describe him to police as dressed in khaki washable slacks, a sport jacket, well-kept brown hair, about six feet tall, weighing about 185 lbs, and possibly wearing glasses – although, despite numerous interrogations under hypnosis, she could never be sure if he had glasses or not. Her description produced the less detailed sketch of the man suspected of being the killer – the one that was initially released by police.

Uafinda remembered more specific details about the man when he was hypnotized. He recalled that the man was dressed "like a gentleman," and that he had khaki pants, boat-style sneakers, and was well built, being neither fat nor thin. He also recalled that the man wore a tie, had glasses, and wore a plaid button-down shirt under his tan sport jacket. The man led Erdley into

31

the Core, pointed out the body of Betsy Aardsma lying on the ground, and left. Erdley began trying to check the girl for a pulse or signs of life.

Uafinda, feeling something was amiss, began to follow the man up the stairs. As they reached the desks at Level 3, a student employee of the library described seeing a man with glasses rushing out of the library, with a black man seemingly chasing him. Her description produced the sketch of the man wearing horn-rimmed glasses, with somewhat unkempt hair. Once outside, in the gathering darkness, the man in the tie outpaced Uafinda and disappeared in the direction of Recreation Hall.

Erdley was having little success assisting her classmate on the floor of the library. Books lay everywhere, and a few metal shelves had been knocked loose from their supports in the fall that Aardsma had taken. Her red dress, with a white turtleneck underneath, had some spots of blood on them, almost invisible on the red dress, and the two were standing in a puddle of urine, involuntarily released by Betsy during the shock and trauma of whatever had happened to her.

What Erdley didn't know – what no one knew – was that her friend had been stabbed once through the heart. Erdley began to scream for what she later described as "ten to fifteen minutes," although in reality, based on timelines provided by other witnesses, it was likely much less than that.

Uafinda wandered back through the Core, then the man who had been sleeping at the study carrel near them came in. One of the librarians, Patricia Bland, sprinted up to level 3, where receptionist Elsa Lisle called for an ambulance at 5:01 PM. The Ritenour Health Center dispatched a pair of student paramedics, telling them that a girl had fainted in the library. George Miller and Gerald Titus were competent paramedics, and when they arrived they noticed that another library employee was giving Betsy mouth-to-mouth resuscitation.

After parting the small crowd that had gathered around the fallen girl – a crowd that included the overcoat wearing, mustachioed man that Shirley Brooks had passed on the steps while returning Betsy's pen, the paramedics began their work. One felt that he could feel her pulse, and the other finally noticed the drops of blood on her dress. They placed her on a collapsible gurney and removed her through the service elevator on the Eastern side of the Core.

33

Marilee Erdley was visibly shaken by the event, and she gathered Betsy's white coat, the Africa book, and Betsy's purse from the assigned graduate study carrel where Betsy had left them on Level 3, then headed over to see Betsy at the Health Center. Later, she would be found rifling through Betsy's purse as she waited in the Health Center for her friend, who would never return. When asked what she was doing, Erdley snapped out of her daze and replied "I don't know." She was completely unaware of her actions since the moment she saw the body of her friend lying on the floor of the Level 2 Core.

Once at the Health Center, Miller and Titus continued CPR, giving chest compressions in the time-told manner in which they had been taught. Dr. Scott Pilgrim was on duty that night, and he noticed blood oozing out of her chest with each repetitive compression. Something more was wrong here. He ordered the two young men to stop giving compressions. Pilgrim, the supervising physician at Ritenour, declared Betsy dead at 5:19 p.m.

In the library, the process of cleaning up had already begun. Someone on the library staff had ordered janitors to clean up the urine in the aisle and

34

stack up the books and fallen shelves neatly. Someone had fainted or fallen, and the library had to be cleaned up and the scene properly dealt with. None of the library employees had reason to suspect a murder, so no one thought it unusual to clean up the hard tile floor to prevent slipping or further damage to the books that had already fallen there, which included *Schizophrenic Germany* and a number of other works about medieval England and France.

Outside the library, students leaving Willard Building reported hearing sirens around 5:00-5:10 PM. Most thought it odd, because the campus was almost entirely deserted that weekend, but beyond that, little attention was paid. One student who had heard the sirens returned to his residence at Beaver Hall, about a ten-minute walk from the Willard Building. On his floor, only four students out of the hundreds who might normally be there remained that weekend. Two were working on research, and the other two were members of PSU's Blue Band who had stayed for a band function.

At dinner that evening in the dining hall after 6:00 PM, someone told him that there had been a murder at Pattee, but he and his remaining friends laughed it off. Surely, this was a prank or false information. Later on, as he studied in the lounge at Beaver Hall, one of the three students on that floor came in and told him he had heard via a telephone call that a grad student had been murdered in the library.

No one in the group of friends at Beaver Hall knew the name of the girl who had been murdered that night. The student recalled that he did not learn her name until the following day, when he went downtown to purchase a newspaper.

Meanwhile, Pennsylvania State Police officers were beginning to arrive at the Pattee Library to take charge of the situation. At that time, there were two local security forces -- Campus Security, which controlled the overall campus security operation; Campus Patrol, who escorted students between buildings at night and kept order – and a town police force, the State College Police Department, which lacked jurisdiction on the campus.

The Pennsylvania State Police, who responded to the call for help, were stationed at that time at the Rockview Barracks, right outside the State Prison at Rockview, about fifteen minutes from the town. Like the college students they protected, most of the State Police were away on Thanksgiving vacation. Sergeant George

Keibler, who would remain on the investigation for many years, returned early from a bear hunting trip the day after the murder to assist Lieutenant William Kimmel with the investigation.

The first man on the scene, Trooper Mike Simmers, was an undercover drug investigator and part-time university student. He instructed Campus Patrol officers to secure everything and begin removing students from the library, which they did, posting guards who would stay there all night. It was a lengthy process, taking place across multiple floors, and in most cases, no one who had not participated in the event was aware that there was anything unusual happening.

Even as late as 7:00 PM that night, Campus Patrol would report breaking up a couple having sex on another level of the stacks. By 8:00 PM that night, Dean Brungart would receive a call from the police telling him that a girl had been murdered that night. Police did not arrive at David Wright's apartment in Hershey until around midnight, where they told him that his girlfriend was dead.

Once the attending physician at Ritenour cut away Betsy's blood soaked bra and blouse, and he and Trooper Simmers saw that there was a stab wound

37

present, Simmers declared it a homicide and called back to the Rockview Barracks, requesting any other available officers who could help. He bagged and tagged Betsy's clothes as evidence and began the initial procedures of opening a homicide investigation. No one was sure what had happened or why, but the machinery that made up the Pennsylvania State Police was moving into action.

The police had their work cut out for them -- between 4:30 and 5:15 PM, the foot counters at the library doors recorded that roughly 440 people came into or out of the facility. 440 potential witnesses. 440 potential killers.

Everything was operating smoothly that might, at least after the moments in the Core when a strange man barreled through the rows of books, asked for help for a girl on the floor, and then left as quickly as he had come. The last twenty minutes of Betsy Aardsma's life were almost surreal in the calmness that surrounded them, and the following few hours saw a general return to normalcy at the college. Students went about their business as if nothing had happened. The police shook off the late fall chill to begin the investigation of the first murder of a University student in 28 years.

Autopsy of the Aardsma Murder

The autopsy of Betsy Ruth Aardsma would be conducted the night of her murder at 11:00 PM, at the Bellefonte Hospital in Bellefonte. Her body was transported to the Hospital by the coroner, the autopsy was scheduled, and the physician was called. Dr. Thomas J. Magnani was selected to do the autopsy that night, and he appeared at the hospital, ready to perform the sad task of identifying fully what had caused Aardsma's death.

Today, Thomas Magnani is a grandfatherly figure with a soft-spoken demeanor and an impeccable fashion sense. In his eighties, he still looks the part of a physician, with a crisp bow-tie, slacks, and a button-down shirt as his usual attire. He stays active, too, playing tennis at the same athletic club as some of the retired State Police officers who worked on the Aardsma case. His memory is as sharp as his wit, and he recalls the Aardsma murder very well.

"There was nothing [in the results] that suggested a struggle of any kind," Magnani recalled, almost forty years after the fact. He believed that she must have known her killer, and that he approached without causing any alarm on Betsy's part. While he was certainly no expert; not a trained killer or assassin, as many people believed, "the guy knew what he was doing" when he aimed for her heart. This was no accident – the assailant was doing his level best to ensure that his attack was permanent. These facts are seared into the elderly pathologist's recollections, perhaps because of the memories that are associated with them.

* * *

In 1969, Magnani was a young physician just starting out. He had performed autopsies before, but some of the State Police were skeptical about whether or not he could handle the task of correctly performing the Aardsma autopsy.

A dispute broke out, with the police arguing over whether or not Magnani should do the job. Finally, he left in disgust, returning later when they called him back and implored him to come do the autopsy. As Magnani recalls, he was still upset, but agreed to do the job – and he billed the State Police for both trips he had to make to the Bellefonte Hospital that night.

The autopsy began around 11:00 PM, and would not conclude until 4:00 AM. Magnani supplied his own camera, with color film, to take pictures for his autopsy file, while the State Police used a black and white camera to document the proceedings for the police file. In addition, the whole procedure was recorded on a record-player style recorder – an expensive device that Magnani supplied himself, which would cut an actual LP-style vinyl record of the proceedings.

Unfortunately for understanding what transpired that night, this recording seems to have been kept at the Bellefonte Hospital, and was likely discarded or archived when the Bellefonte Hospital closed and was replaced with a new hospital near Beaver Stadium on the grounds of the Penn State University.

A call to the Records Department of the new hospital was met with a terse answer, delivered quickly and without much searching on the part of the Records Officer – "Those recordings were destroyed," she answered, after half a second's pause on hold while she checked for them. "So they were destroyed, you're sure?" I asked. "They would have been, yes." Just like that, the matter was closed.

* * *

In his autopsy, Magnani found Betsy to be in good health and for the most part uninjured, beyond the "penetrating stab wound of the chest." The wound:

> Traverses the subcutaneous tissue and muscle and enters the anterior sternal surface three inches inferior to (below) the sternal notch. The wound completely traverses the bone at the level of the third rib. The sternal wound measures 7/8 of an inch in length. The pericardial incision measures approximately ¾ of an inch in maximum length. The wound in the pulmonary artery measures ¾ of an inch and it has an inverted "V" shape."

In short, the knife had penetrated her breastbone, pierced her heart, and nicked her pulmonary artery, causing her to bleed out into her chest cavity – making her unable to scream; drowning her in her own blood.

The part of the autopsy report that caused the most consternation, both to investigators and to Magnani, was the irregular petechial hemorrhaging evident in the bruising on the chest. Some of the police felt that the killer had worn a large wristwatch on his wrist, and the force of the attack had caused the bruise. Magnani himself initially felt that the mark was a sort of suck mark or hickey, perhaps caused by an intimate encounter the night before between David and Betsy. For his part, Wright denied having given Betsy a hickey.

Petechial hemorrhages are most commonly seen in the eyes of victims of strangulation or asphyxiation, where they are caused by tiny capillaries bursting due to pressure and lack of oxygen. When found on the body, as was the case with Betsy's murder, they are often a sign of pressure that has been applied to the body, causing the bursting of the small blood vessels below the skin.

Petechial hemorrhages can occur either while the victim is alive, or in some cases even post-mortem. In Betsy's case, the hemorrhages could have been caused by one of two factors – the blow of the butt of the killer's hand as he drove the knife into her chest, or by chest compressions performed by passersby or the Ritenour paramedics as she lay on the floor of the library prior to being removed in the ambulance.

Aside from this, and the minor abrasions and bruises around her ear that most likely resulted from her fall into the bookshelves of Aisle 51, there was nothing unusual about Aardsma's autopsy. The conclusions of Magnani were that she had been approached from the front by an unknown right-handed person or persons and stabbed. Death had occurred within minutes, and she was unable to scream or otherwise talk because she bled out into her chest cavity – essentially drowning in her own blood.

The Return of View filed by Coroner W. Robert Neff was terse and to the point.

> *On November 28, 1969, Betsy Ruth Aardsma, age 22, of 117 E 37th St., Holland, Mich., a graduate student at Penn State University, living at 5A- Atherton Hall on the Campus, was found lying among the stacks on the second level of Pattee Library. She was taken by ambulance (University) to Ritenour Health Center where she was pronounced dead at 5:20 p.m.*
>
> *An Autopsy held at Centre County Hospital by Dr. Thomas Magnani revealed the cause of death to be Intra Plural Hemorrhage due to Stab wound of Chest.*

This office ruled the death Homicide by person or persons unknown.

Strangely, the information in the Coroner's return of view conflicts with the Centre County Hospital records from the autopsy, which state the time of death as 5:50 p.m. Where the thirty minute discrepancy comes from is unknown, but the hospital records would seem to be more accurate, as they were filled out prior to the autopsy, while the return of view was not typed up and signed until December 3, 1969.

A few months later, in March, the autopsy report was filed with the Centre County Prothonotary's office – an odd decision, and perhaps an accident. Nothing else about the Aardsma case has been made public, aside from a few photographs and some general police sketches of the man thought to be the killer. Why such a sensitive document made its way to the dusty but otherwise public filing drawers of the Prothonotary's office less than five months after the murder is still unknown.

The Days After

The following day, the Centre Daily Times picked up the story. The Daily Collegian was closed for the break and would not feature its first story on the murder until the following Monday. The news quickly spread, being syndicated in numerous papers around the country, but it took second billing to news of the Manson family murders, which had happened a few months prior, in August 1969, and which were finally beginning to see arrests and progress being made.

The newspaper reports varied drastically, with some papers reporting luridly that the girl had been found "in a pool of blood," and that a "shrill scream" had emanated from the stacks prior to the appearance of the first man on the scene, neither of which was true. Confusion also occurred because the police reported that they were looking for "two men." This came, not just from the information provided by Brungart, but because Uafinda had left the scene after unsuccessfully following the suspect out the door. Police were looking for two men – Uafinda and the man he had followed. Richard Allen had also not immediately come forward, because neither he nor Uafinda suspected anything nefarious had occurred.

Lt. Kimmel, acting as head of the investigation and spokesman for its progress, kept tight-lipped on the police activities and the theories that they were working on. Among the ideas floated to the press over the next few weeks were the main theories that have remained constant over the years. These main theories include the idea that Betsy had witnessed some act, either a homosexual encounter or a drug deal, that had led to her death; the idea that Betsy had been attacked by a mentally imbalanced individual, who may or may not have been a University student; the idea that Betsy had been targeted because of her alleged involvement in modeling for the art department, and the idea that Betsy was randomly targeted for any number of reasons.

Among the potential theories that were passed around among students and faculty at the time were that Aardsma had been a drug informant for the police or FBI, that she had been stabbed with an ice pick, and that she had been killed by a transient who had been passing through town on the recently-completed Interstate 80 and had been overcome with an urge to kill. There was even a rumor that Aardsma was the first

47

victim of a serial "Alphabet Killer," who had targeted her because her Dutch last name placed her as the first person in the 1969 student directory. The police did nothing to discredit most of these rumors, preferring to keep silent as to what they were considering.

Most of the early police theories centered on the idea that Aardsma had been murdered by a classmate from English 501. This was due in part to the large number of English 501 students who were circulating the library that day. In reality, this was not unusual – the same large final project that had caused Aardsma to return from visiting her boyfriend in Hershey was weighing heavily on the minds of many of her classmates, and plenty of them had come back to meet with Meserole or to work on research of their own in preparation for the project's due date.

Betsy's friends Linda Marsa and Rob Steinberg were interviewed, as well as her roommate, Sharon Brandt. Aardsma's diaries, which she had kept fastidiously since she arrived at Penn State, were examined, but provided little in the way of insight into the crime. Aardsma had been a devoted girlfriend and a spotless student, spending most of her free time studying in her room, and her diaries showed no trace of any unusual activity. In the words of one of the original investigators on the case, "There was nothing in her diaries that you wouldn't be ashamed to show her parents." Her personal effects would be returned to her family, along with the letters she had received from her boyfriend David Wright since she had arrived at Penn State.

The only mention of anything unusual came from Betsy's roommate. Betsy had apparently lost her key to their dorm room recently, and this was part of the reason she and Brandt were planning to meet up after her time at the library – she couldn't get back into her room without Brandt being present until she had obtained a new key. Another strange thing was Brandt's mention to investigators when asked if there was anyone that had come around that she felt they should talk to. Brandt mentioned the name of Richard Haefner, saying that he had visited a few times and spoken with Betsy. Beyond that, she couldn't remember anything about the tall, brown-haired geology student.

Over the next few days and weeks, pieces of the puzzle would begin to come together. Allen and Uafinda would come forward and be interviewed by the police. Uafinda, who had the double misfortune of being both black and a foreigner in 1969, was looked at especially closely and received numerous interviews under hypnosis, but he was completely cooperative. He and Erdley were subjected to a number of hypnosis interviews under a licensed hypnotherapist named Dr. Philip Domin, who was flown in at police expense from Hazelton, PA.

Uafinda's cooperation, and the fact that he and Erdley had been near enough in the stacks to look at each other after hearing the crash also helped to move suspicion away from the young Geography student from Mozambique. In interviews and statements, Kimmel pleaded with students and faculty to come forward with information relating to anyone who had "behaved suspiciously" the night of the murder or during the days afterwards. No one did.

At that time, the college was lord and master over its employees, and rocking the boat was not looked upon kindly. Had any employees, or even students, pushed the issue, or implicated the college, it could have led to the loss of academic standing, jobs or access to pensions and retirement funds for anyone bold enough to do so. If you were going to stick your neck out on the line, especially about the Aardsma murder, you had better be certain that you were right, and prepared for what might come.

Assistant Stacks Supervisor Dean Brungart experienced this very phenomenon personally. One of the pictures that came out a few days after the murder in the local papers was of Brungart, his tall, muscular frame partially hunched over in the stacks, half-smiling as he pointed to an aisle similar to the one Aardsma had been murdered in. He had agreed to pose for the cameras, but doing so nearly cost him his job – he was quickly reprimanded by his supervisors for appearing in the photo.

Police did not interview Haefner based on the information provided by Brandt for several days to a week following the murder. When Trooper Ken Schleiden first met him, Haefner was seemingly concerned and helpful, offering to tell police what he knew. He had met Betsy on the front steps of Atherton Hall, where they both lived – she in 5A with her roommate Brandt, and he in room 64. He had been in room 48, he related, but he had requested a change to a private room for reasons he did not share. He recalled that Betsy was writing a letter when he saw her, and the

51

two struck up a conversation that led to several dates in late October.

Haefner told police that they had gone for ice cream at the Creamery, where students in the agricultural sciences division who were learning to make and sell ice cream provided their tasty wares to the public. They had also gone bowling together at Bellefonte Lanes, facilitated by Haefner's old white Ford Falcon, which he shared with his brother George, but was allowed to borrow from his parents in Lancaster if he gave enough notice. Additionally, they had gone for dinner at the Nittany Lion Inn.

Following that date, according to Haefner, they had plans to take a car ride together, but one or both of them had been ill, so they had cancelled their proposed date. By the end of October, Betsy had called off their budding relationship, citing her intention to remain seriously involved with David Wright. He remembered specific dates that their meetings took place, and he seemed well-prepared for his interview.

Haefner also told investigators that Aardsma had related certain information to him that he could only have known had she told him – information that was not released in the media for nearly forty years after the murder. He told police that Betsy had once had a knife pulled on her in Ann Arbor, and that she had come to Penn State to get away from the depredations of the Ann Arbor serial killer, John Norman Collins, who was murdering co-eds near the University of Michigan campus where she had been studying.

He also told police that he had been eating dinner at the HUB Student Union building on the night of November 29th when he found out about the murder, and that he had felt physically ill when he discovered that his former girlfriend had been murdered. As far as the Pattee Library? Well, he never went into Pattee, he told police. He did all of his work at the Deike Library, where geology materials were kept elsewhere on campus, to which he had a key and unlimited access.

Notably, he did not mention visiting Lauren Wright on the night of the murder. Years later, Wright recalled that on the night of the murder, as his family was sitting down to dinner around 6 p.m., Haefner had arrived at his house in a panic. "Have you heard?" He blustered. "A girl I dated was murdered in the library." He sat down with Wright and spoke to him for a time.

After he left, Wright and his wife were left with the distinct feeling that Haefner may have been involved in

53

the incident he was describing. There was just something about his mannerisms and excitement. Of course, it is difficult to imagine one of your students committing murder – so Wright dismissed his own suspicions as unreasonable and chose not to report it to the authorities at that time.

Without this important piece of information, police at the time had no reason to suspect Haefner – he was a strong student and a reasonably personable young man, clean cut and on his path to a Master's degree in Geology. There was no indication that he had been in the library that day, and no indication from his personality of strong feelings or any anger towards Betsy.

Trooper Ken Schleiden, who performed the initial interview, cut him loose that day, preferring to focus on the classmates or the theory that someone much closer to Betsy had been involved in her murder. The State Police would bring him back a second time in the spring of 1970 to be interviewed by a Criminal Investigative Specialist, a higher-ranking officer who specialized in ferreting out details. Apparently, he told a largely similar story, with a few minor changes that did not set off any alarms in his interviewer's mind.

The police continued to talk to the media and tell them of their lack of suspects, and to assure them that everything possible was being done. What the police held back from the media was almost as shocking as what they were unaware of. In a small corner of the Core used for storage of desks and spare shelves, only a few aisles over from where Aardsma was killed, detective Mike Mutch had found a desk with a half-empty can of soda and a collection of adult magazines. Obviously, someone had been there, and had been interrupted in their leisure. The magazines, a mixture of homosexual and straight pornography, as well as soft-core girlie magazines with titles like "Mr.," "Bachelor," and Frolic," full of lurid stories and bikini-clad models (similar to "Maxim" magazine today) were found in the pile.

In 2008, Trooper Mike Simmers recalled reaching up above a shelf to the left side of the aisle where Betsy had been killed and pulling down a hardcore homosexual pornography magazine that had come from Amsterdam. He also recalled that there were other pornographic magazines found stuffed between books elsewhere in the Core. Clearly, there was reason for police to believe in their homosexual *coitus interruptus* theory.

To assist with the limited forensics available to them in 1969, the police brought in Mary Willard, a diminutive female professor from the University who had helped them in the past. Willard was known for her groundbreaking work in the field of chemistry. She had lived in Moffat Cottage on the campus grounds prior to the founding of the school, and had been born there in 1898. After graduating Penn State in 1921, she returned there to work, even helping to solve a crime when consulted by police in 1931.

Though short in stature, Willard's experience and access to forensic equipment made her an important assistant to the state police. She arrived in the Core bearing an ultraviolet "black light" that she used to detect the presence of minute amounts of bodily fluids at crime scenes. This was cutting edge technology in 1969, and what she and the police found was astounding.

The Core stacks in the aisle where Betsy was killed were covered with semen – or at least material that would show up under black light exposure. Certain kinds of soda, such as ginger ale, will fluoresce under UV light, so it could be that the core was simply messy. Willard and police came to a different conclusion. Dried semen was everywhere, coating the floors, the walls, and even some of the books as high as the top shelves. Willard collected samples to use for possible serotyping, an emerging technology that would later help to convict Ted Bundy, by detecting the blood type of the individual who had left the semen at the scene.

Unfortunately, there were no true DNA tests available in 1969, and so little was done with the samples beyond serotyping to determine if the blood type of the donor was secreted. Furthermore, most of the samples were dried and likely several days old, if not older. The crime scene was a mess, and the presence of pornography, semen, and the Coke can further complicated an already confusing investigation.

Investigators discovered another interesting piece of evidence, on the Eastern side of the stacks, near the stairs leading up to the Level 3 Core. A spray of tiny blood droplets, similar to how water would spray if you flicked your hands against the wall before toweling them off after washing them, appeared oriented vertically on a wall near a light switch at the stairs and indicated that someone had passed there. It had not been the paramedics – the stairs were far too narrow for their gurney, so they had used the service elevator on the west side of the Core.

This blood, which was tested and found to be Betsy's blood type, had to have come from the killer as he exited the building. Now police knew that the man who had told Erdley that "that girl needs help" while hiding his right hand at his side – the man who Uafinda had chased out of the library into the night -- was not just a helpful Good Samaritan or potential witness – he was the killer.

Police did say that they had no reason to believe that Aardsma had been followed and that there was little to suggest that this had been a planned attack, given the nature of the crime, the rapidity of the assault, and the choice of location. Her boyfriend, David Wright, was quickly cleared of being a suspect – he had been in a study group with other med students at Penn State Hershey at the time of the murder. There was little to suggest any truth to rumors of Betsy's involvement with drugs, and there was no mention of any other jealous suitors in her diaries or among her friends. With the main "usual suspects" in this type of crime already eliminated, the police had no choice but to begin the grinding work of interviewing hundreds of college students.

The campus granted the State Police the use of the Boucke Building as a temporary command center, which quickly filled with 20 to 30 police officers working in teams to begin interviewing classmates, other students, faculty, staff, and anyone who might chance to come forward with information. During the last week of English 501, students recalled that pairs of investigators came to the room and began pulling students in pairs to interrogate them separately from their classmates about their knowledge of Aardsma and their whereabouts that day. Right from the start, Betsy's entire class of nearly 60 students was interviewed, along with others who had been on campus that day.

One of Betsy's classmates had aroused the suspicions of both Professor Joukovsky and the Pennsylvania State Police. Earl Ryan Martin[2] was a thin, blonde young grad student of average height when he first arrived in Joukovsky and Meserole's English 501 class that fall. He caught Betsy's eye, or at least held her interest long enough to take her to coffee on at least one occasion. His interests were much more primal

---

[2]   Name has been changed.

than most of his classmates – knives, hunting, and outdoorsmanship ran high among his hobbies. In the very anti-war, anti-conservative Sixties, students like Martin stuck out like sore thumbs.

Despite being interviewed by the State Police after Aardsma's murder, and possibly even subjected to a polygraph test, Martin was cleared of being a suspect and went on to turn his Penn State degree into bigger and better opportunities. After spending some time in the military overseas, Martin eventually took a job with a government intelligence agency – and it was here that he would come back on to the radar of the Pennsylvania State Police.

According to a former Crime Beat reporter for the Centre Daily Times, Martin had failed a routine polygraph test that was administered as a part of his top-secret clearance – a normal occurrence for a government employee of his stature. The question that had tripped him up had been a simple one: "Have you ever been part of a felony investigation," or some variation thereof. For whatever reason, his mind wandered to being questioned in the Aardsma incident some thirty-five years before, and he failed the polygraph.

The administrators questioned him as to why he had failed and when it was discovered that he had been questioned in the Aardsma murder, the Pennsylvania State Police were notified. Many of the officers have strongly believed that Martin is a viable suspect, but despite numerous polygraph tests and interviews, as well as his complete cooperation in questioning, there has never been anything concrete to tie him to the crime. At best, the story goes, he was "twenty feet away" when the murder took place. He cannot or will not recall further details.

In the world of many police officers, polygraph tests are an important investigative tool. Pennsylvania Law does not allow them to be admitted as evidence of guilt or innocence. As one trial judge put it, "the polygraph is a fanciful notion, and should be viewed as such." Despite a large amount of evidence from studies that show that polygraph tests are ineffective at best, there is still a great deal of believe by police officers in these "scientific" indicators of guilt and innocence. As a result, there is speculation that Martin may have been involved in the Aardsma murder.

Looking at the facts, however, it seems unlikely at best. Martin was a thin, blonde student, with a similar build to Aardsma; certainly not brutally strong enough to deliver the blow that would take her life. Furthermore, he went on to lead a life inseparably tied to government intelligence – meaning that he would be subject to frequent psychological and polygraph examinations. The fact that he has failed one of these examinations does not automatically mean that he killed his former classmate.

One of the most important problems with the idea that Martin killed Aardsma is that the killer left the core and spoke with Marilee Erdley – a classmate of Aardsma – taking the time to lead Erdley to Betsy's body. How would it be possible that Erdley would not have noticed that she was being led to Betsy by a student in her own English class – not to mention one with such an outsized reputation that he was still remembered distinctly by Professor Joukovsky, forty years later.

I spoke with Martin in the summer of 2011, asking if he'd consider meeting for lunch. "I'm afraid it would be a waste of your time," he said. "I remember very little about what happened that day. The police have interviewed me a number of times, and I haven't been able to give them anything useful." Whatever Martin knows, he cannot or will not recall it now.

* * *

Beyond the interviews and on-campus presence, the police also went above and beyond normal investigative procedure for a crime of this scope, searching the campus from top to bottom. Since the murder weapon had not yet been found, police were anxious to see if it had been discarded by the killer elsewhere on campus. Some officers were assigned to search the rooftops of every building on campus, while other officers emptied every trash can on the college grounds, rifling through them in hopes of finding a bloody knife, clothes, or some other scrap of evidence that could prove useful. On the first floor of the Core, in the men's restroom, a small penknife was found behind a toilet and was duly entered into evidence. It was later determined to be too small to have been the murder weapon, and did not prove useful to the investigation.

These early efforts proved ineffective. No murder weapon was found, and no smoking gun that could implicate someone as the killer appeared. The killer had either outwitted them in hiding his blade, or had taken it with him and discarded it somewhere unknown to anyone but himself. Christmas, 1969 came and went; another class of students left for break and came back, and the investigation dragged into the spring of 1970 with no leads, no suspects, and no real information. The police kept interviewing people, kept working on every possible lead, but not much information was forthcoming. The press went on to cover new stories and new incidents, and police statements started to come sporadically, then only on anniversaries.

Based on media reports, the public picture of the crime that was emerging at that time was of a random, chance encounter. No one among Betsy's friends or acquaintances on campus had given any indication of being a crazed killer. The investigation was a race against time at this point, or maybe a waiting game. Something would surely come out sooner or later. Meanwhile, Aardsma's family flew out from Holland, Michigan, to collect her body and her personal effects, then returned to her hometown for her funeral services.

As Time Goes By

Betsy's funeral was held in Holland, Michigan, a few days after the murder. At the service, her pastor stated that Betsy's death was "God's will." Her family and others were in attendance, including her boyfriend, David Wright. Initially, Wright hadn't wanted to go, but his parents convinced him that he should attend. Betsy was viewed in an open casket, holding a single red rose – Wright and his parents sent an additional dozen roses. She would be buried in the family plot at Pilgrim Home Cemetery in Holland, Michigan.

In an attempt to generate leads, Penn State offered a $25,000 reward for information leading to the arrest of Aardsma's killer, but beyond that, they had little contact with the family. Esther Aardsma recalled years later that they had never heard from anyone at the college after the murder, and that she felt disappointed that no one cared enough to follow up. They had sent their daughter away to Penn State to get an education, only to have her return in a casket.

For the most part, despite the drug culture, the anti-war sentiment, and the protests, Penn State

University was a reasonably safe place to be in 1969. Campus Patrol was available to escort students to and from classes, and well-lit paths were available for students who chose to travel alone at night. Campus Security, headed up by Col. William C. Pelton, a World War II veteran and staunchly conservative right-hand man to Eric Walker, University President, took a hard line, Old Western attitude towards keeping the peace on his campus.

In the year leading up to the Aardsma murder, between September 15, 1968 and February 11, 1969, there had been nine assaults on female students on the Penn State Campus, and thirteen incidents involving exhibitionism. Despite the fact that female students were held to a curfew, while male students were allowed free roam of the premises, there were still occasions where young co-eds found themselves in danger. Some of these incidents were run of the mill robberies and attacks, while others were frightening and strange.

One example of such an incident involved a young female teaching assistant to Dr. Charles Kolb, working as a graduate with his Intro to Anthropology class in the spring of 1968. One of the male students in the class had developed a fascination with his young female teaching assistant. He would spend time coming to visit her during office hours, and his unusual demeanor and attention to the young female teaching assistant concerned Kolb, who recalled loitering outside her office to make sure everything was alright until the student would leave, even going so far as to walk her home one night to her apartment on Beaver Street. The student, who she described as socially remote, had always been aloof and distant, but his attentions had begun to turn disturbing.

At some point, the student's attentions turned strange and potentially violent. Having apparently stalked her to determine where she lived, he appeared at her apartment one night around midnight or shortly after in sweat pants and a top, out of breath and sweating as though he had run a great distance. He smiled at her when she opened the door, but said nothing, finally exposing himself to her. He wasn't aroused, she recalled, and the whole event didn't seem sexual in any way. She turned her back to him.

"I won't look at you until you make yourself decent," she said, at which point he climbed up the flight of stairs in front of her apartment and crouched down to stare at her. She asked him to leave, threatening to call

the police. He left at that point. The following day, a
German language professor, Jacques Rose, appeared at
her door, nervous and excited. He took her aside and
explained that a student of his who he had lunch with
that day had told him that he planned to kill his female
professor. Rose had done some research and found
that she was the only female professor listed on the
man's schedule. He had looked her up and rushed to
her apartment.

Jacques Rose was from the State College area,
and had attended college as an undergraduate there,
graduating in 1963 with a degree in German. In 1965,
he had helped raise money for Dr. Martin Luther King
Jr.'s civil rights activities in Birmingham. By 1967, he
had received a degree in Comparative Literature and
become a professor at Penn State. He was pleasant, but
had a strange affect about him, and many of his
students felt that he may have been homosexual.

Rose had reported the matter to the Dean of
Students, and they asked her to leave her apartment
until the young man was caught. He would not return to
his dorm for three days, after which time he was
arrested and, according to what Rose later told her, was
institutionalized for schizophrenia. Later that summer,

the woman got married and moved away from the University, and by 1969 she would not have been anywhere near State College. She wondered, though, if the man might have developed a similar fascination with Aardsma; an obsession that perhaps turned violent.

Although she was in contact with Kolb periodically, and had discussed the case and her strange experience with the student with him, she had not seen or spoken to Rose in many years. She was certain that he could provide the name of the student, since he and Rose had been close. She remembered that it was very unusual in academic circles that an undergraduate student would have lunch with a professor back in those days, and the student may have been a graduate student, or may have had a personal or intimate relationship with Rose, based on her feelings that he was a homosexual. She asked me to put her in touch with Rose if I ever found him, so that the two could catch up.

I contacted Charlie Kolb, who works in Washington, D.C., and he recalled the incident, but not the name of the man. His course was a college requirement, meaning that even post-graduate students who entered or transferred into the college would have to take the class if they did not have some similar coursework on their transcript. Nearly anyone could have been in the class, which had attendance figures of up to two hundred students in some cases.

I searched for Rose or any family members that might recall him or his whereabouts for a number of weeks before, on a hunch, deciding to look up an address listed for him in 2001. I had been unable to find a phone listing for him at that address, although it was still listed as current. Searching the address online revealed that it was a nursing home in the Bronx. There had to be some error, I thought. I dialed the numbers and, when the receptionist answered, I asked for Jacques Rose. I was told that I would be transferred to the nurse in his unit.

"Mr. Rose is unavailable to speak with you." A thickly-accented Hispanic woman informed me. "Will he be available later on?" "No." "What about tomorrow?" "Mr. Rose will never be able to speak with you. He has been in a coma for years now. We think he can hear, but he cannot respond to anyone."

I thanked the nurse and hung up. The Rose trail was at a dead end, and the only man who might be able to remember the specifics of the incident or the name of the student was lying comatose in a nursing home.

A retired police officer recalled to me that a schizophrenic "townie" – a young male who was not a student at the University, but a State College native -- was interviewed regarding the Aardsma murder, and later cleared. All he could recall was that the man's last name began with the letter "A."

Colonel Pelton maintained a gruff disconnection to the incidents taking place on campus. "I think that some girls report that they were assaulted when actually they weren't, just to get a little attention," he told the Daily Collegian in a 1970 article. Women were also at fault for "inviting mishaps" by "walking through parking lots and other unlit areas, instead of on lighted sidewalks." He went on to blame revised visitation rules for males in female dorms for some of the problems on the campus. "Now it's almost impossible for us to control who's in the dorms, and when."

Despite the changes made since the Aardsma murder, which included the addition of a single full-time investigator, a single full-time patrolman, and a single part-time patrol officer, Pelton warned that future assaults could occur.

In the same article, the Pennsylvania State Police investigation, still led by Lt. William Kimmel, revealed that "between 2,500 and 3,000 interviews had been conducted with University staff and students," but that "no concrete evidence had yet been uncovered." Kimmel remained tight-lipped about what little evidence police had uncovered up to that point.

With so much at stake, President Walker was not about to leave the investigation of the Aardsma murder up to the State Police. Walker was a hard-nosed Englishman who had lived most of his life in York, Pennsylvania, before taking up engineering at the suggestion of one of his high school trigonometry teachers. Turning down a Penn State degree for a Harvard education, by 1945 he had returned to Penn State as a part of the Ordnance Research Laboratory, where torpedo and ultrasound research took place.

Walker was appointed University President in 1956 – hand-picked by then-president Milton Eisenhower, the brother of then-president Dwight D. Eisenhower. During his years at the University, Walker would be instrumental in growing the college – including overseeing creation and growth of the Hershey Medical

School where Betsy's fiancée David Wright was training to become a doctor.

Cancelling his plans to attend Penn State's showing at the Orange Bowl, Walker and his right-hand Security man, Col. Pelton, began an investigation of their own into the possible killer or killers of Betsy Ruth Aardsma – an investigation that started with his own personal "shit list."

In a truly Nixonian touch, University President Eric Walker had created and maintained a list of individuals, organizations, and events that had been harmful to the college, whether physically in terms of actual damages, or in terms of loss of standing or bad press towards the University. Among the individuals Walker had his eye on were members of the Black Student Union who had barricaded themselves inside a building during a Vietnam War protest and had damaged some doors in the process, and a number of professors who had made statements against the college. When he stepped down in 1970, the murder of Betsy Aardsma was still at the top of his "shit list."

Whatever the results of Walker and Pelton's investigation, they were unable to solve the murder themselves, and their files, if any, have been lost to history. It has been rumored that more information exists, even a possible file, but no proof of these documents has come to light. Whatever the motivations for his personal crusade to find Betsy's killer, the regret that must have been felt by Walker is palpable as one considers that he was one of only two University Presidents in history who had to turn over the reigns of the massive organization with blood on his hands.

As the days and weeks after the murder turned into years, the police force working on the case dwindled from the twenty or more officers assigned to the Boucke Building to a single investigator or a pair of investigators working from the Rockview barracks. Within a few months after the murder, with the majority of their interviews and investigative work complete, the State Police gave their temporary office at the Boucke building back to the college. By 1972, the reward offered by the University had expired, unclaimed. No one had come forward with anything substantial, and police were largely without leads to go on or angles to pursue.

In the spring of 1970, one last possible break would come in the case. A young boy waiting outside the Recreation Hall for his mother, who had brought him to work with her that day to visit the campus, uncovered a knife under one of the bushes. The knife fit the size and shape of the murder weapon that police were looking for. They turned the weapon over to the Campus Security officers, but it is unclear what became of it from there. If the State Police at Rockview have the weapon, they have not spoken about it. Unfortunately, any fingerprints or DNA evidence that may have been on the knife had likely been long removed by weather, snow, and ice as it sat under the bush.

On April 20th, 1970, students stormed the President's Mansion at the eastern end of the Hintz Family Alumni Center as part of a political protest, causing the University to rethink the safety of having the President live on campus. Eric Walker was the last of the University Presidents to live on the actual campus proper.

In July of 1970, John Oswald took over the reigns of the Pennsylvania State University. His son, John Jr., was in ninth grade that fall, and remembers his father talking about "what an awful tragedy" the Aardsma murder was, both for the family and for the reputation of the college he was now leading. John Jr. also remembers running through Pattee Library on a number of occasions by himself as a young man of fourteen or fifteen, and despite the concerns his father had about the tragedy, he was never warned away from spending time in the library stacks.

As senseless and seemingly random as her death was, Betsy's murder would prove to be cataclysmic in other ways. Her death, and the rising crime on campus in the early 1970s, would lead to the creation of a University Police force. No longer would Campus Patrol and Campus Security form the thin line between law and order, backed up by the Pennsylvania State Police. Instead, a full service University police office would be established, leading to improved safety and security throughout the campus.

Betsy's sister Carole Aardsma became a minister, and would go on to testify before the Supreme Court when the constitutionality of the death penalty came up in 1972. She stated that "Betsy would not have wanted her killer punished by death," sharing the religious viewpoints that she and her sister had been raised on.

As class after class arrived, studied, and graduated from the college, the Aardsma murder slowly faded into memories and rumors – a story to scare incoming freshmen, and a secret that the college wanted to bury. Events would take place in the following years, though, that would suggest either that the killer was still among those at the college, or that someone with a sick sense of humor was not going to let the University forget.

On February 22nd, 1977, a letter arrived at the office of the Campus Police, addressed to Sgt. George Keibler at the Boucke building. This was incorrect, of course – the office at the Boucke building had been closed for years, and Keibler was a State Police officer. The letter was postmarked from Atlanta, Georgia, and bore no return address. When the letter was opened, the shaky handwriting revealed a message that was vile and shocking:

> *"You never did catch the guy who killed that cunt in the library back in '70, '71, did you? Well fuck you all! Here's a present for Washington's Birthday you'll never forget!"*

Unfortunately, when the letter was dusted for prints, it was found completely smudged, with no usable prints present. The handwriting was also unusual – it appeared as though the letter writer had purposely tried to conceal his handwriting, or was incapable of writing properly for some other reason.

77

What was the significance of this letter? The date was not an anniversary – indeed, while the holiday was now called President's Day, the letter was referring to Washington's Birthday. President's Day had not been officially declared a holiday until the Nixon Administration. So the message was anachronistic, and angry. Police investigated alumni in the Atlanta area but there were far too many to link anyone to the letter, and besides, Atlanta has long been a hub of regional air traffic, so anyone flying or driving into the town could have dropped the letter in the mail.

Despite these gruesome reminders of the Aardsma murder, Oswald did the best he could to lead the college forward and away from the tragedy he had inherited from the previous administration, but he was never able to put the capstone on the Aardsma investigation, and he left the college a dozen years or so later without the resolution that Walker and the rest of the administration had been seeking from the beginning.

In the years after the murder, the college took steps to prevent would-be visitors to the core from visiting the scene of this unseemly chapter of Penn State University history. The core stacks were re-numbered, with the Level 2 core becoming "Stacks BA" – some say in memory of Betsy Aardsma. More lighting was added to the core, and some of the bookshelves at the end of the aisles were removed. The flooring remains the same as it was in 1969, and many of the graduate study carrels are still painted in the drab olive green that they wore in 1969. Most of the numbers have been removed, so it is hard to tell where Betsy's study carrel was. For the most part, the University had succeeded in forgetting the Aardsma murder, aside from the occasional anniversary article that would come out in the Daily Collegian or the Centre Daily Times.

After the taunting letter, the next eerie reminder of the Aardsma murder would come in the form of a shrine found in the core stacks in 1994, around the 25th anniversary of the killing. Stacks Supervisor Tom Whalen found a candle burning in Aisle 51 on December 3rd, 1994. Around the candle were scattered old newspaper clippings of the Aardsma murder, and written in red marker on the floor In front of the macabre display were the words:

R.I.P. Betsy Ruth Aardsma, Jul. 11, 1947 – Nov. 28, 1969. P.S. I'm Back.

Police were called, and photographs were taken, but again, no one could be linked to the display. The candle was still burning, so it was likely that the shrine was not more than a few hours old. Police had long since removed their hidden cameras from the stacks, placed there after the murder in hopes that they could catch suspicious activity if the killer had returned to his crime.

The date is troublesome – if it was the killer, had he forgotten the day he had murdered Aardsma? Or had he been otherwise occupied and unable to make it up for the real anniversary? Perhaps it had just been a sick joke, played by a fraternity brother, or an imbalanced individual. The possibility exists that it was an elaborate prank – the Library Special Collections building has a file on Aardsma that contained original clippings and information, but most of those original clippings are no longer there. Although you are required to sign out the collection to view it now, things may have been different in 1994. Whatever the source, the shrine was quietly cleaned up, and library employees were instructed not to talk about it.

Some secrets can't or won't stay buried, though, and in 1999, around the time of the 30th anniversary, another shrine was found. This time, the bizarre display was set up in the wrong aisle, and the marker used to write on the floor was blue. The newspaper clippings included with this shrine were photocopies. This shrine was generally considered to be a copycat, as it appeared so obviously to be a fake. No further shrines have appeared, despite the passage of the 35th and 40th anniversary. Either the killer has died or is no longer commemorating his activities, or the pranksters no longer feel that the joke is funny.

The Drug Burn

One of the prevalent rumors making the rounds across campus in the days and weeks after the Aardsma murder was that Betsy had been working as an undercover drug agent, or some type of informant, and had been figured out and silenced by the drug dealers and users on the Penn State Campus. The rumor seems to have originated from the rapid response of the State Police to the crime, as well as to the fact that one of the first officers on the scene, Mike Simmers, was actually an undercover drug enforcement investigator.

Drug use on college campuses was a problem throughout America in the late 1960s, and Penn State, despite being a more conservative environment than many Universities, was no different. The Pennsylvania State Police were busy with undercover drug busts, which resulted in numerous large busts on an almost weekly basis throughout the late 1960s. Marijuana in the 1960s was starting to come into its own as a drug of choice for the "hippy" generation, and it was not uncommon for drug deals to take place in and around the sprawling University campus as students tried to free their minds and open the doors of perception.

In most cases, published reports in the Daily Collegian and elsewhere describe mild circumstances for students arrested with marijuana. Mandatory sentencing laws were not yet in place across most of the country, and in many cases, a slap on the wrist or a potential suspension from the University were the worst possible outcomes that would happen. As was the case at most universities across the country, many Penn State students were openly critical and antagonistic towards the drug policy of the PA State Police, as well as that of Penn State University, as evidenced by a letter to the Editor of the Daily Collegian published in 1968:

> I don't think I'll be letting the cat out of the bag (nickel or dime) by mentioning that there were narcotics arrests made in State College this past week. (How pot makes it as a narcotic is beyond my understanding, perhaps it taxes your credibility also – but don't take my word for it, ask any narco and he'll gladly bust you.)
> Steve, Saul, and Al (the writer's friends) were arrested for the alleged possession, use,

and sale of marijuana. I don't know whether this happy crew was selling (as the police would have us believe) this drug (as the police would have us believe) that is threatening to shake (as the police would have us believe) America to its foundations (Read a newspaper lately? Shake? The foundations need dynamited).

This all-powerful little item grows as a weed with little or no care. Its leaves are cured like those of tobacco and indeed, after it is cut it resembles high grade tobacco. It is rumored that when its smoke is inhaled it produces a feeling of joy, happiness, contentment, and love. I have heard no reports suggesting that marijuana causes cancer, heart attack, baldness, menopause, or nepotism.

Are they guilty as accused? Guilty of what – being happy, selling happiness? This may be illegal, but is it a crime? While the super-human crew is at it, why don't they put a shadow on all those students who might possibly be guilty of premarital sex (Love is a crime too, you know).

Let's run virginity checks on all the co-eds!
Spare no expense! Someone, somewhere, may
be happy.
– Robert Thomas '68

In reality, the PA State Police were employing undercover narcotics agents, such as Trooper Mike Simmers, who were students at the college while fulfilling their police duties. The goal was to catch potential drug users, buyers, or dealers, and to uphold the Pennsylvania narcotics code. This they did, quite effectively, while also providing a presence that could prove useful in other occasions. The fact that Trooper Simmers was able to respond rapidly to the Aardsma murder is one such example. Having a police officer around, especially in a turbulent college environment at the height of anti-war, pro-drug, and other demonstrations, can be quite handy. Of course it could also lead to rampant suspicions and the potential for angry diatribes, as evidenced by the letter to the editor.

Col. Pelton, the head of Campus Security, flatly told the *Daily Collegian* in an article on the Campus Security department in 1970 that "we are not actively looking for people who smoke pot. We're more concerned with getting the pushers." He also denied wiretapping of student phones, and the use of paid informants, while admitting that Campus Security did work with federal agencies to try to apprehend known dealers. "If a person attends, say, a festival in New York, and is known to be headed for Penn State, we are notified by the authorities and once he arrives here he is put under surveillance by narcotics agents."

There is little evidence to suggest that Betsy was an undercover informant, but the genesis of the drug rumor can be found in Betsy's FBI file, which is surprisingly thin, containing only a few pages of requests from the early 1970s for cooperation between the Philadelphia Bureau offices and the Pennsylvania State Police in requesting information on similar murders or crimes that may have happened on college campuses after the Aardsma murder. One or two similar cases are outlined here, which were eventually resolved and attributed to other suspects who could not have been in the State College area on November 28th, 1969.

The contents of this file appear to be more the result of investigators grasping at straws as the murder passed three, four, and five anniversaries without a suspect than anything else. The file contains nothing to suggest that she was working for the FBI, or that she had any governmental involvement at all. She certainly wasn't working for the State Police. What the file does contain, however, is the story of one of her classmates who was arrested for drug possession a few years after the murder.

The classmate, whose name is redacted, had dropped out of Penn State shortly after Aardsma died. He had been serving in the National Guard in State College, and had joined the regular army after becoming disillusioned by the death of his friend. A few years later, he had been busted for having a small quantity of marijuana while on base. A Sergeant of the Pennsylvania State Police at Rockview requested his file from the US Department of Defense via the FBI, and the file was provided to them.

Even the FBI, though, felt that this was an extreme long shot. The file states plainly that:

> The Sergeant advised that he personally feels that this individual should be considered a prime suspect in this killing, even though there is no strong evidence to support his contention.

Obviously this rumor, while seriously examined for a time by the officers in charge of the Aardsma murder investigation, was never taken seriously by anyone outside of a few select police officers who had their hearts in the right place, but were looking in the wrong direction. The focus on one of Betsy's classmates as the killer had seemingly caused them to become myopic in their search for the truth. Why they had thought that Marilee Erdley, also one of Betsy's classmates and the individual approached by the suspected killer, would not recognize one of her own classmates approaching her in the core that day, has never fully been explained.

There were other cases that the State Police were interested in, including then-unsolved homicides in Alexandria, Virginia; Austin, Texas, and Philadelphia, Pennsylvania. None of the cases they inquired to the FBI about were ever linked to the Aardsma murder. The case was unique and did not seem to be linked to a repeat offender.

In addition to the drug rumors, stories had circulated that because Betsy's father was a higher-up in the government in Holland, Michigan, she had been killed as a hit to penalize her father for some decision he had made, or some business partner he had upset. This made little sense and was quickly dismissed along with the drug rumors, by police and eventually by students. While Betsy's father did work for the government in Holland, Michigan, he was a sales tax auditor for the Michigan State Treasury, not in a position where he would have been a likely target of attacks on his family.

Of all of the theories put forth by the police in the 1960s to explain Betsy Aardsma's murder, the drug theory seems to be the least potentially plausible of all. However, they were doing their best to examine every possible angle, and it would have been remiss of them not to consider the possibility that drugs were involved. As far as anyone has ever uncovered, her dalliances into substance usage were limited to sneaking cigarettes on occasion with her friends outside Atherton Hall.

Perverts in Pattee

The Pennsylvania State Police were not being unduly prejudiced when they suspected that witnessing a homosexual encounter or an exhibitionist act could have led to the violent murder of Betsy Aardsma. In the late 1960s, homosexuality was still classified in some circles as a mental illness, and being accused, convicted, or otherwise charged with homosexual acts could seriously impact an individual's potential future career options or even their college standing. So it was plausible to the investigators that the interruption of a homosexual liaison could have been a reasonable motive for murder.

An excellent example of the potential for problems that could arise from being known outwardly as a homosexual in the late 1960s and early 1970s can be found in the case of Joe Acanfora. Acanfora, a freshman student in the education department at Penn State in 1968 who had graduated as Valedictorian from his high school in Brick, NJ, was also openly homosexual. He wanted to teach earth science at the high school level once he graduated. His activities at Penn State included becoming one of the founding members of Homophiles of Penn State, and acting treasurer, in 1971.

The University moved to squash the fledgling gay rights group by refusing to officially recognize the organization, and Acanfora and the other members threatened legal action, which resulted in the recognition by the University, but also the public acknowledgement of Acanfora's sexuality. This public recognition was the root of Acanfora's problems. When he attempted to finish his education degree in 1972, Dean VanderMeer of the Penn State College of Education openly questioned whether or not he should be able to become certified as a public school teacher, asking openly whether a homosexual could fulfill the requirement of "being of good moral character" that is required of a public school teacher in Pennsylvania.

On July 28th, 1972, three years after the Stonewall Riots at a gay nightclub in Greenwich Village – largely accepted as the beginning of the gay rights movement as it is known today, and which had occurred in April of 1969, only seven months prior to the Betsy Aardsma murder -- Acanfora appeared before a panel of all six Deans of the Penn State College of Education,

91

presumably to answer the question of whether or not he possessed sufficiently good moral character to achieve certification in the state of Pennsylvania. The transcripts of this panel appearance are filled with the prejudicial and stereotypical views held by many in the 1960s regarding homosexuals. A short excerpt shows the nature of some of the questioning:

> Dean VanderMeer: Then, I would like to ask further: What homosexual acts do you prefer to engage in or are you willing to engage in?
>
> Acanfora: Which homosexual acts?
>
> Dean VanderMeer: Yes, which acts of expression of love, as you put it, for male friends?
>
> Dean VanderMeer: An additional question on this particular topic: Do you look for other males with which to have sex?
>
> Acanfora: I would say that's a question very similar to the one just discussed.

Dean Sharon: Do you feel, as a gay person and being involved in love relationships with men, that you are any more promiscuous . . .Do you uphold by that tenet that gay people are more promiscuous in public than heterosexual couples?

Acanfora: This is a common myth just like the myth that homosexuals are somehow attracted to children and that homosexuality males are all effeminate. There are so many myths connected with homosexuality because of the lack of opportunity to educate on the subject, and this is just one more that homosexuals are promiscuous - will go out seeking sexual activity with anyone they can find - and it just isn't true. It's just another myth that is connected with homosexuality because of ignorance on the subject.

In the end, the Deans were gridlocked, and they passed the matter of whether or not to certify Acanfora to the Pennsylvania State Secretary of Education. John C. Pittenger did not certify him immediately, and

Acanfora went on to teach in Maryland, where he was fired for not stating on his employment application that he was a homosexual after it came out in a press release in September 1972 that he had been officially certified by the Pennsylvania Department of Education. He sued the Montgomery County School District for wrongful termination, His case would later go all the way to the United States Supreme Court, which denied certiorari but which nevertheless helped to establish the rights of gay teachers.

Acanfora had openly admitted his own sexuality through his threatened lawsuit against the University, which was part of the reason he had run into problems. In 1969, however, gays at Penn State who wanted to remain in the closet communicated through the use of an underground newsletter, "The Water Tunnel," named for the Garfield Thomas Water Tunnel that runs in a 257 foot rectangular loop under the Penn State campus and had been used for classified military research, including the testing of torpedoes and other underwater weaponry, since its completion in 1950.

For entertainment, the My-Oh-My night club was the preferred homosexual meeting place in State College, and in fact was the only gay bar in the area. The

My-Oh-My, owned by Jack Sapia, was actually two bars in one. In the front, a small section of the bar was used as a gay bar, while a separate larger portion in the rear of the bar was a go-go style topless bar employing a variety of semi-famous girls from Pittsburgh and Philadelphia. Depending on your sexual preference, you would enter the bar either through the door to the left or to the right – leading either to the gay bar or the strip club. It was often rumored that you could meet interested gay males by sitting on the wall that faced the front door of the club and watching who came and went, but to solicit sex in public was a dangerous pastime.

The My-Oh-My achieved a dubious notoriety in 1970, when a bikini-clad woman with the words "My Oh My" stitched across the top and bottom of her skimpy outfit rushed across the field at Beaver Stadium just before the Penn State versus Navy game commenced with its coin toss. At that time, it still stood out as a place where college students over 21 could go to drink, meet other men for casual encounters in relative privacy, and not be judged for their sexuality.

Pattee Library itself was also noted for its share of homosexual encounters and other, more disturbing, deviant behavior. "The library was...a den of perverts,"

95

Sergeant George Keibler recalled. He then mentioned the case of an older man, a local dentist, who enjoyed visiting the stacks and sitting at the study carrels there. Once he had sat for awhile, he would soil himself, then sit in his own feces and watch until he could attempt to convince a pretty coed to come over. After he had aroused the attention of a suitable female, he would tell her that he had had an unfortunate "accident," then give her money and ask her to run out to buy him a pair of underwear so that he could change. He was well known by the Police and Campus Security officers who would occasionally have to cite him after an uneasy coed would report the incident to them.

Jose DeJesus[3], the exchange student from Colombia that had passed Shirley Brooks on the stairs when she returned Betsy's pen, was another one of these known or suspected perverts. While he had no police record, his presence had been reported by a number of jittery girls who said that he had followed them around the darkened stacks, or had lurked in aisles nearby while they researched, unnoticed to them until he accidentally made some sound or motion that had called attention to his position. His leering glances

---

[3]   Name has been changed.

could have been mistaken – perhaps cultural differences were to blame for his lengthy stares at these attractive girls – but his brown overcoat made him seem more like a flasher or a peeping tom and less like an innocently misguided exchange student.

Campus Security at one point had DeJesus under photographic surveillance, and it was from this surveillance that police were able to identify DeJesus. Although they were aware of his reputation, and despite the fact that a witness had positively identified him as being present in the library on the day of Betsy's murder, the State Police for some reason never spoke with DeJesus, who returned to Colombia to pursue teaching once he received his degree in 1971.

A former female student at Penn State relayed another strange story of the Stacks. While descending the stairs in the stacks one evening, a male passed her coming up the stairs. In the narrow confines of the stairs it was impossible to pass someone without turning sideways, which she did – at which point the male student punched her as hard as he could in her chest, then shoved her away and ran up the stairs and away before she could catch her breath. Odd behavior continues in the stacks to this day. In 2008, Penn State basketball player Stanley Pringle was arrested and charged with masturbating in the stacks as he sat behind a female student and attempted to initiate a conversation with her. Reports of individuals defecating on books are also common.

In the 1960s, certain areas of the library had also gained a reputation of their own as places to find action any time of day or night. The Level 1 Core, in the very basement of Pattee, was a preferred meeting place for random homosexual encounters. In the days before Craigslist and the internet, homosexuals looking for a thrill would meet there and summon each other underneath the stalls for sex. The problem grew so bad that the library officials had to remove the stall walls and doors in the Level 1 Core bathroom to prevent some of the behavior. It was not uncommon for men to "hang out" in the bathroom, styling their hair or eyeing visitors until they found someone suitably attractive or acceptable to their advances.

For those homosexuals who were more discreet about who they met, other methods were available. One method was to place a note inside of a book, then write the call number of that book in a corner of one of the stalls. The person who noticed the numbers and looked up the book would find a note describing the writer's age, body type, and preferences, and a way to make further contact or a time to meet if the finder was interested. Although library officials regularly cleaned the bathrooms, these call numbers did not arouse much suspicion when written in sufficiently small letters in the back corners of the stall.

If prospective homosexuals failed to make a connection at the library, there were alternate locations for meetings. Another popular homosexual spot, active mainly in the afternoons, was the basement restroom area of the Carnegie Building, which had been the original university library prior to the construction of Pattee. At the time, the Carnegie Building, home of the Journalism Department, was sparsely populated, and with its six booths in a row, was a private spot to meet and engage in homosexual activity. In the evenings, the janitorial office nearby made it unsuitable for use as a meeting place.

When meeting for sex, the usual restroom code among gay males was to tap their foot while watching the response of the man in the next stall. If the response was positive, notes written on scraps of toilet paper could be exchanged, leading to the eventual meeting in a mutually agreeable location. Because it was dangerous to be "out" as a homosexual at that time, face to face meetings were uncommon, and most gay men were not openly friendly to one another, for fear of being suspected as homosexual.

The Campus Patrol was aware of the status of the various restrooms as meeting places. In the ancillary areas of the Carnegie and Sparks Buildings, it was not uncommon for a time to hear cries of "Campus Patrol, queers, clear out!" This approach was not used in the Pattee restrooms, however.

Heterosexual encounters were not uncommon either, as evidenced by a story of a couple having sex on the Level 1 Core and being removed by campus patrol the night of the Aardsma murder. However, at that time, only the homosexual encounters taking place there would carry the stigma of potential ridicule, expulsion, or future career issues. The story told by Dean Brungart about seeing two men standing a few aisles away from Betsy and talking quietly, perhaps even lurking, added credence to this idea. The Coke can at the desk, along with the mixture of straight and homosexual pornography found at the desk and in the aisles, also seemed to lend an air of truth to this scenario.

Investigator Mike Mutch felt that Betsy had seen the two men having sex, had potentially recognized one or both of the men and been recognized by them, and had been startled. He felt that the men had quickly gotten their wits about them and decided that they had to silence her before she ruined one or both of their careers. His belief was that they chased her into the aisle and roughly stabbed her, allowing her to fall against the shelves while they left. Not everyone in the State Police shared this theory, however, and for equally good reason.

Would Betsy have merely blushed and gone about her business if she had run across two men engaging in sexual acts in the Core? Also, having been accosted before with a knife while at Ann Arbor, would she have merely stood quietly while someone approached down the aisle and threatened her? Had she felt that she was going to be attacked, she surely could have screamed, and there were several people close by who could have heard and responded. Finally, if they had given chase, why had she allowed herself to be cornered in a dead-end aisle, with no possibility of escape, and why had she not run at least to the very end of the aisle before being subdued?

101

How had no one else noticed the pair of men
pleasuring each other in the core earlier? Shirley Brooks
had said that she and Betsy were alone in the core,
except for the two men who had been there earlier.
When she had returned the pen, there was no one else
present. No one seemed to report hearing any moans of
pleasure or any unusual sounds that might accompany
two men having sexual relations in the quiet library
stacks. Even though some of the pornography, including
the hardcore Amsterdam magazine was recent – dating
from October and November 1969 – it was possible that
it had been placed there for easy access during a
planned or unplanned future encounter, or had been left
there unnoticed by library staff for days or even weeks
prior to the murder.

The mentality of the hypothetical homosexual
killers has to be examined as well. If they felt that they
had been recognized, they would have to assume that
Aardsma would tell someone, therefore potentially
affecting them. They may have tried to reason with her,
tried to talk her out of reporting what she had seen, or
tried to downplay the significance of it.

Mr. Allen only heard one man talking to one
woman from his vantage point at the copy machine just

prior to Aardsma's murder. What possible outcome could have been so bad for the killer or killers that they felt that murder, and all of the potential for personal problems, arrest, and even a death sentence that it carries, could have been preferable to a slap on the wrist sodomy charge, or the potential for a lesser conviction or castigation for homosexuality?

Finally, where was the second man, and how did he leave the Core? It seems that only one man exited, running around the northern part of the greater stacks and exiting near Uafinda and Erdley on the Eastern side. Had there been a second man, he would have been noticed by someone at some point during the events that unfolded that day.

The magazines and Coke can discovered by investigators that led to the suspicion that homosexuals or deviants were responsible for the murder of Betsy Aardsma were examined and dusted for prints. Partial prints were found on the soda can, but they have never been matched to any individual in police databases. With no serious suspects, the State Police did not take the time to print all of the students they interviewed, either, so no comparison prints from her classmates or friends were available. The prints on the magazines were limited, and according to retired investigators, the few prints that were retrieved were smudged and unusable.

Perhaps the killer enjoyed a soda and a magazine while he sat in the Core the day, but more than likely, the soda and magazines were a red herring, left undisturbed by someone either earlier in the day, or on a previous occasion.

Until these facts were revealed, it had never made sense from the news articles why, with what little evidence they had released, the police would suspect homosexuals were involved in the Aardsma murder. Now it made perfect, logical sense.

The Frustrated Artist

Another fascinating individual whose name surfaced as a suspect came in the form of Bill Spencer. He and his wife, a graduate student at Penn State at the time of the murder, had allegedly thrown a party where Bill bragged about killing "that girl in the library" and had attracted the attention of the Pennsylvania State Police. Bill had been arrested for growing marijuana, and he and his wife lived in an old schoolhouse on Waddle Road at the time of the party where he had bragged about the murder to an assembly of English faculty and staff.

According to the people who had related the story to the State Police, Spencer had claimed that Betsy had modeled nude for him – a bold statement that seemed out of character for her, but that fit with some early rumors that had made the news about her being involved in modeling. At the time, nude models for the art department were brought in from Philadelphia, though – there was no such thing as a student nude model in the PSU Art department.

* * *

William Cleveland Spencer was born in March, 1929, in North Carolina. Little is known of his early years of life, except that he came late to his college education, beginning to attend the Boston Museum School of Fine Arts at the age of 27. He attended from 1956-1960, then again from 1962-1963. His wife, Nancy – a much younger woman, was born in Rhode Island in January of 1944, and attended Skidmore University right after graduating high school.

They found themselves relocating to State College around the same time as the Aardsma murder. In December of 1969, Nancy was attending Penn State as a philosophy major, working on her Ph.D. in Philosophy. The couple had married a few years prior in Star Island, New Hampshire, and had been living in Boston where William – or Bill, as he was known to almost everyone – had taught sculpture at a local college. Nancy had been accepted at Penn State, and Bill had been offered a job teaching sculpture there that would support them while she finished her Ph.D.

Things had been looking up for the Spencers – right up until the marijuana bust. Bill had been growing a small quantity of marijuana in the backyard of their home, an old church on Waddle Road, just outside of State College. Somehow, the police had found out, and he was arrested and charged. Word spread quickly, and soon the offer to teach sculpture at the University was rescinded, leaving Bill unemployed and briefly unable to support himself and Nancy while she attended college.

The couple was used to hard times and strange circumstances, though. Even Bill and Nancy's relationship had been the product of secrets and lies. Bill, along with his first wife, Lena Nargi, had been the proprietor of a little coffee shop in Saratoga Springs, New York, near Skidmore University that they had opened together in May 1960.

The Caffe Lena, now the oldest continuously operating coffee shop in the United States, was started with little more than a wing and a prayer by Nargi, the daughter of Italian immigrants, and Spencer, the charismatic sculptor who attended the Boston Museum School of Fine Arts as a student and part time instructor. Married in 1958, the two devised the idea of the coffee shop as a way to entice Skidmore students to spend a little money and pick up a little jazz and folk music culture, as well as a being a profitable business venture that would allow them to retire early and travel through Europe while they were still young.

The Caffe Lena struggled mightily for the first few years of its existence. Despite their dream of providing up and coming folk acts with a start, the Skidmore crowd wasn't terribly receptive to the music being played at the Caffe. Lena and Bill were instrumental in getting Bob Dylan his first two performances as a favor to their friend, folk artist Terri Van Ronk. The two-night 1961 show he played at the Caffe Lena went so poorly – the audience was loud and largely ignored Dylan -- that Bill Spencer climbed onstage to chastise the crowd of college students:

> *"You may not know what this kid is singing about and you may not care, but if you don't stop and listen you will be stupid all the rest of your lives. Listen to him, dammit."*

Bill's angry diatribe had little effect, and Dylan left Caffe Lena the second night as unknown as he was when he first arrived on stage. Bill quickly became disillusioned with the coffee shop, the closed-minded clientele, and the Saratoga Springs area.

Whether out of frustration with the boorish college audiences, the stagnant economic conditions at the Caffe, or for other reasons, Bill was actively pursuing other interests. While instructing at Skidmore, Bill had met Nancy, a freshman who was easily swayed by the attractive, charismatic, artistic and hip Bill Spencer, who told stories of his time overseas and of his coffee shop business – a man described by friends as "energetic and charismatic," and who could "sell ice in Antarctica."

In 1962, Bill Spencer left Lena and the Caffe to pursue his relationship with Nancy, seeming not to care about leaving his business and his marriage behind. Nancy must have known what she was doing when she got involved with him – she kept their relationship a secret from everyone, and even her family did not learn of her relationship with Spencer until she was named as a party in the divorce proceedings filed by Lena Spencer.

Having claimed at various times to Nancy's family and former coworkers that he was a "soldier of fortune" who had served with the United States Army in Korea prior to being an infantry instructor in Fort Bragg, North Carolina, and even an assassin, working freelance for the Israeli military at some point, Bill had come late to the world of academia, mainly on the strengths of his talent for sculpture. Now, he began to take odd jobs doing home remodeling and assisting their neighbors and friends – most of them professors at Penn State – with their work around the home. He also began working on remodeling their church home, turning part of it into a sculpture studio.

Just up the road from the Spencer residence was the old Boogersburg Schoolhouse, a one-room school that had been closed in 1953 and which had been purchased and remodeled into a studio by noted sculptor Sybil Grucci, whose bronze bust of Fred Pattee still adorns the lobby of the library that bears his name. This small area outside of State College proper was a fertile ground for artists, English faculty, and other professors, and Bill Spencer – with his talents for sculpture, his connection to the University through his wife's scholarship there, and his home improvement skills – soon found himself in high demand as a handyman and friend of many of those professors and artists.

While working for the local cadre of professors who lived nearby, Bill began to establish a reputation as a bit of a braggart. No one was quite sure how much of his background was truth, and how much was

110

embellished. Michael Begnal, an English professor at the time, recalled that one day he had been working with Bill on some carpentry at his home near Waddle Road, where Bill and Nancy's home studio was located. He had looked up from under the cabinet where they were working to see Bill standing above him, holding a hammer – and with the most chilling, blank expression on his face. According to Begnal, it felt "like he could have killed me right there." Begnal never quite got over that impression of Bill Spencer, and others in the English department shared the nameless dread of Spencer that Begnal had felt, even forty years after the fact.

Another professor of English, who spoke on condition of anonymity, related one specific incident at a Christmas party in 1969 that convinced him that Spencer may have been involved in the Aardsma murder. He recalled that he and a number of other professors and students had attended a Christmas party at a farmhouse owned by one of the English faculty that year – a party where Bill had circulated amongst the crowd, commenting on the murder. Bill had made several shocking claims, including the fact that he knew Aardsma, that she had modeled nude for him to sculpt in order for her to make extra money, and that he had been in the library that day. He spoke of his alleged training in the special forces, going so far as to say "It would be so easy to have killed that cunt," among other disparaging remarks. His reputation among the English department, as well as his inflammatory comments that day, were sufficient for Spencer to draw the attention of the Pennsylvania State Police the following spring.

Bill Spencer was 41 years old when he was brought into the Pennsylvania State Police's temporary office at Boucke Building in early spring of 1970. His story had not changed much since the Christmas party where he had ranted about Aardsma, but he had done a bit of polishing. Spencer told police that he had known Aardsma, and that he had been in the library that day. He also told them that he had seen the killer, and was willing to produce a bust of the man he suspected of killing Aardsma.

He mentioned a swarthy, overcoat-wearing man who was known to frequent the library, and who had been seen that day – Jose DeJesus. When police cut Spencer loose after his initial interview, he promised to return with a sculpture of the killer, and return he did – with what must have been a masterful bust of DeJesus, coming from a man who had been awarded the Albert

Whitten Memorial Scholarship in Sculpture from the Boston Museum School of Fine Arts.

The police were underwhelmed – dismissing his story as well as his work on the bust. He continued attempting to convince them to take him and his "evidence" seriously, but their take was that "he was a nut." Spencer was angry – at the college, the police, at the Art Department for rescinding his employment offer, and presumably at the English professors who worked for and whom he suspected had reported him to the police. There wasn't much he could do except continue to work odd jobs and steam about his treatment in State College. This he did, telling anyone who would listen about how he had been treated unfairly and how he had given police a perfect description of the killer, but they had been too stupid to listen to him. What became of the bust is anyone's guess, as the police never took it into evidence.

Despite Spencer's claims, there is no evidence that exists to suggest that Betsy Aardsma ever posed – nude or clothed – for any art or sculpture classes, and there is no reason to believe that she had ever met the Spencers. Their late arrival to the Penn State area in 1969 leaves little time for Betsy to have encountered either of them, and the fact that Nancy was studying Philosophy while Betsy was majoring in English leaves little overlap between their areas of interest.

It also seems that Bill was never contacted again by police after 1970, despite his strange reputation amongst the English department. Also, aside from his marijuana conviction, which resulted in a small fine and a summary judgment, Spencer spent the period between 1969 and 1973 without committing any other crimes.

Nancy graduated in 1973, and she and Bill relocated to Richmond, where she had been offered a job at Virginia Commonwealth University, teaching with the English department. Bill made a tidy amount of money when they sold the old church, turning a profit of around $20,000, so the two had seed money to begin their new life in Virginia. There is little evidence to suggest that Bill ever worked again, and it is seems clear that if he did work, it was as a handyman like he had been in State College.

The two lived in Richmond from 1973 to 1979, while she taught at Virginia Commonwealth University as a professor of linguistics. Bill again made a name for himself among her co-workers, being known as a friendly, outgoing man, who bragged about his time in

114

the service and his experiences in Korea and as a Drill Instructor at Fort Bragg. During this time, Bill's health steadily worsened – he was nearing fifty years old, and he had one or more small heart attacks that left him in poor health.

These heart problems – and Bill's incessant stories of danger and intrigue -- were remembered by several of Nancy's colleagues at VCU. Neighbors at the Waddle Road address also recalled hearing of his heart problems, so the Spencers must have kept in touch. Nancy's family lived in Atlanta, Georgia, only a few hours' drive from Richmond, and she and Bill may have visited them during this period – perhaps in 1977, when the taunting letter was mailed to the Pennsylvania State Police.

At some point after 1979, Bill and Nancy Spencer divorced. No one seems to know the reason why, and the records of their divorce are legally sealed in the state of Virginia, accessible only by the parties involved, or by immediate family members with a legitimate interest in the proceedings. Bill Spencer seems to have returned to his native North Carolina, where he passed away in 1984, probably of another heart attack. Nancy, however, continued to work on scholarly articles with her former colleagues at VCU before meeting Earl Austin, a man who everyone knew as "Doc." She and Doc abandoned academia and the East Coast for Arizona, where Nancy worked as a telemarketer for the Nielsen Group. Almost 20 years later, they moved to Sarasota, Florida, where they spent about five years before ending up in a trailer park in a small town in North Carolina in 2006 about three hours away from where Bill Spencer had died.

* * *

According to her surviving family, Nancy, the only person who might have known whether Bill was involved in the Aardsma murder or not, and her new husband Doc had lived a strange life in their last years together. Never having had children of their own, they adopted a young pregnant couple who were in distress, allowing them to live in their Lumberton home with them. The couple disappeared after a few short weeks, and within a few months, Nancy was dead, at the age of 64.

When I tried to find "Doc," the story got even stranger. Doc Austin, who had no family of his own; who was prone to Bipolar Disorder and who enjoyed dressing

116

in women's clothing and carrying around an urn filled with his late wife's ashes, woke up one morning in November of 2008, a few months after his wife's death, and walked out the front door of his house, leaving the television on, the door open, and his cell phone on the coffee table. He has never been seen or heard from since. Neighbors reported the door open a few days later, causing police to investigate.

I spoke with the Sheriff's office in charge of handling the missing person case for Earl Austin in early 2010. In a thick southern drawl, the Sheriff asked me if I was "kin" to the Austin's. I replied that I wasn't, and related the story of Nancy's first husband and his strange behavior as a reason for calling. Without going into details, the Sheriff sighed and told me:

> "It's the strangest thing. It's like that boy disappeared off the face of the earth. We've been lookin' for him for two years, and never found a trace. We took dogs all around the woods and fields and never got a hit. He left the cars, his keys, everything – he can't have gotten far. But what we found inside the house, that's what was really strange. Those people, they

117

were...they were livin' some kinda double life.
Weren't what it appeared. Very strange..."

The trailer has since been sold at auction, and all traces of Earl and Nancy Austin presumably relegated to sheriff's auction, the evidence locker, or the dumpster. Earl Austin has never been found, and Nancy's family, who had little contact with her after her divorce, provided no evidence as to why she left teaching and was on the move. Was she afraid of an ailing and angry Bill Spencer? Or was she simply looking for new challenges outside of academia? It's likely that we will never know the whole truth.

What is known is that Bill Spencer was never considered a serious suspect by law enforcement in the case. What makes Spencer compelling – besides the fact that his story provides the basis for the nude modeling rumors, is his proximity to Atlanta, Georgia, in 1977, when the taunting letter was mailed to the PA State Police at the old Boucke Building address. Unfortunately, the letter has no usable fingerprints, and is written in shaky, deliberate handwriting that appears as though someone has tried to either disguise their penmanship, or has had strokes or other health problems that prevent them from writing as they used to.

The dates and language referenced in the letter correspond to the time period of Spencer's involvement in the case – *"You never did catch the guy who killed that cunt in the library back in '70 - '71."* – His peripheral involvement with the police was during those years. Perhaps Spencer and his wife visited her family in Atlanta over President's Day weekend in 1977, and he decided to fire off one last shot at the PA State Police and Penn State University.

Whatever the truth behind Spencer and the letter, it had become apparent that the police were correct in their assessment of Spencer, and that he was not the man who murdered Betsy Aardsma. It is my belief that Spencer can be ruled out as a suspect, based on the fact that he does not fit any of the descriptions of the man seen leaving the core, and that from all of the evidence that exists, that he had never met Betsy Aardsma nor had any reason to have come into contact with her.

Sketch of man who said "Someone better help that girl"
as provided by Erdley.

Sketch of man seen leaving the library being pursued by
Uafinda.

Betsy Aardsma as a senior in High School.

Betsy Aardsma as a senior at Hope College, 1969.

The aisle where Betsy was murdered – Police file photo.

Bill Spencer, 1965.

Richard Charles Haefner, lecturing – approximately 1972.

Richard Haefner as Master's candidate in Geology
around 1967.

George Haefner Sr., Rick's father.

Ere Haefner, Rick's mother.

The corner where Rick and Ere argued. To the left is the garage, to the right is 217 Nevin Street, Rick's home.

Close-up showing the corner of the garage area. This is also one of the garages where Rick and his family operated their rock shop from in the 1970s.

Theories Abound

Very few other unsolved cases have the dubious honor of having the Zodiac Killer, Ted Bundy, John Norman Collins, and the Unabomber all associated with them. The Aardsma case has been linked, however spuriously, to all four of these noted serial killers and criminals, in addition to being linked to a professor whose life crossed hers in a number of ways shortly before both Betsy and the professor died suddenly.

* * *

The Ted Bundy rumor was easy enough to source and debunk. One of the investigators on the case, Clifford Yorks, had theorized in later years that Ted Bundy may have been in the State College area in 1969, because that was the year that he had supposedly travelled across the country to try to find his real father in the Philadelphia area. Indeed, Bundy had been born in Vermont, had lived in Philadelphia with his mother prior to their move to Washington state in 1950. At some point in the late 1960s, Bundy allegedly discovered that his mother was not his sister, as he had been told by his family, and that his real father may have lived in Philadelphia or elsewhere on the East Coast. According to Yorks, Bundy had set out to find his real father and may have committed the Aardsma murder on his journey.

There are a number of different problems with this theory. The first is that, by most accounts, Bundy made his trip to the East in the spring of 1969, having been suspected of possibly having committed a double murder that occurred in Atlantic City around Memorial Day, 1969. By fall 1969, he had enrolled in University of Washington and was dating a woman named Elizabeth Kloepfers, whom he dated until 1976. Another problem with this theory is that, when contacted, Ann Rule – a prominent Bundy biographer -- suggested that Bundy had Thanksgiving dinner with Elizabeth and her family that year, and therefore could not have been in State College, committing the Aardsma murder.

Bundy also preferred to kill and savor his time with his victims, mutilating their corpses, molesting them posthumously, and keeping tokens and trinkets from their bodies for later use. Because of this, Bundy also preferred to get his victims alone, and be seen by as few people as possible while committing his acts or luring his victims to help him. In some cases, he would even affect a disguise, such as a cast on his arm or leg, or claim that his car would not start, in an attempt to curry favor and sympathy from his victims so that he could get them to a secluded place where he could murder them. None of these signature events occurred with the Aardsma murder. Furthermore, according to Bundy's own testimony, he did not murder his first victim until 1972, while the first murder linked to him in court did not take place until 1974.

There are plenty of samples of Bundy's prints available, and if any of the prints at the scene of the Aardsma murder had matched Bundy, they would surely have been noticed by the police during one of the many fingerprint database scans that have taken place since then. As dramatic as it is to think that Bundy might have been involved, there is little evidence to suggest that he could have killed Betsy Aardsma on that chilly day in 1969.

* * *

Closer to home, the theory that English professor Robert Durgy may have been involved in Aardsma's death was floated by many in the English Department as well as in the police ranks at the time. Durgy, who had come from the University of Michigan at Ann Arbor to teach English at Penn State University around the same time that Betsy had transferred out of the pre-medical program at Ann Arbor and into the English program at Penn State, aroused suspicion because of his bizarre behavior prior to and shortly after the murder.

Michael Begnal, the English professor who had also known Bill Spencer, had been a confidante of the young professor Durgy, who felt that he could "no longer face his students in class," and who was becoming increasingly agitated and stressed by his workload at the college. Begnal took over some of Durgy's classes for him, and right around Thanksgiving, Durgy finally packed his wife and children into the family car and returned to Michigan. A few weeks afterwards, he was dead – he had driven headfirst into a bridge abutment on a cold, sunny day on a highway near his home – an accident that, when viewed from the road, almost had to be intentional. Durgy had killed himself.

Rumors abounded that Durgy and Aardsma had been having a secret affair; that perhaps she had agreed to meet him in the stacks that day and had given him some piece of bad news – whether it was that she was going to break up with him, or that she was intent on marrying her boyfriend David Wright – that had caused him to finally snap and decide that if he couldn't have her, no one would. These types of salacious rumors are understandable, given the fact that Durgy and Aardsma had both arrived from the University of Michigan at Ann Arbor in the fall of 1969, and that both were interested in English and had ended up in the same department. However, Betsy's letters, diaries, and communications with her friends included no mention of Durgy. Still, police investigated the possibility that he was involved – even traveling out to Michigan to check into things for themselves – but in the end they waited cautiously to hear from Michigan, where police were dealing with John Norman Collins and his Ann Arbor co-ed killings.

Police did not receive word from Michigan until May of 1970, but when they did, they were able to clear Durgy. He and Aardsma had not known each other or had any classes together at Ann Arbor, and there was no evidence that they had met while at Penn State. Durgy was also summarily cleared of being the Co-Ed Killer of Ann Arbor, as John Norman Collins had claimed another victim after Durgy had arrived at Penn State. Collins was suspected briefly as well, but he had been captured in August of 1969, and was quickly cleared, despite Michigan police's fears that the Aardsma investigation might jeopardize their successful prosecution, since Collins had not yet gone to trial for his crimes. Durgy's wife also corroborated the dates that the family left Penn State and arrived in Michigan. Further exonerating Durgy were dated photographs that showed him and his family on Thanksgiving together in Michigan – far away from the core stacks of Pattee on the fateful day that Betsy died.

* * *

One of the most recent suspects in the Aardsma murder has been the Zodiac Killer. A number of internet "sleuths" put forth theories about the similarities between the Aardsma killing and the Cheri Jo Bates murder, which is a suspected, but never proven, Zodiac crime that took place on October 30th, 1966. On the surface, there are some compelling similarities – but again, no evidence has ever been produced that could definitively link the two murders, which occurred three years and three thousand miles apart. The impetus of the Bates/Aardsma connection is a series of desktop poems and taunting letters that were mailed to the Bates family.

In the Bates murder, which took place outside a library in California at around 9:30 PM, was a bloody fight that resulted in Bates ending up dead outside the library, with DNA from her assailant under her fingernails. A few weeks after the murder, police asked everyone who had been there that night to return to the library – and everyone did, with the exception of two individuals: Bates, and the man who had been seen leaving around the same time she did. A military-style watch was found with a broken band near her car, and in the library the following April, a poem was found carved into a desktop that seemed to reference her murder. The morbid poem read:

Sick of living/unwilling to die
cut.
clean.
if red /
clean.
blood spurting,
dripping,

spilling;

all over her new

dress

oh well

it was red

anyway.

life draining into an

uncertain death.

she won't

die.

this time

someone ll find her.

just wait till

next time.

rh

To the casual observer, it seems to make perfect
sense – Betsy's red dress, a second murder, a library,
and a desktop poem. A number of taunting letters were
also sent to the police and Bates' family after the
murder, which somewhat parallels the taunting letters
sent in regards to the Aardsma murder, although there
seem to be no other connections between the letters or
the murders – except one.

One of the alleged pieces of evidence in the Aardsma murder -- one that has only been mentioned by police on one occasion, is a carving found in a desktop that read: "HERE SAT DEATH IN THE GUISE OF A MAN – RSK" Nothing else is known about the significance of this carving, or of where and when it was found during the investigation, but as mentioned before, police scoured the campus looking for any possible evidence, so it is likely that the desktop carving could have been there for months if not years prior to the Aardsma murder.

Whether or not the Bates murder and the Aardsma murder are connected is anyone's guess – but it seems unlikely that the Zodiac Killer, who was actively mailing letters, committing murders, and communicating with police all through October and November of 1969, took a break to come out to Penn State University in order to kill a girl in a library and then returned to San Francisco by December 20th, 1969 in time to mail another taunting letter with a scrap of one of his victim's shirts.

Interesting story, yes – good investigative science, no -- especially when you add the fact that the Zodiac killings and the Bates murder have never been definitively linked by any investigators, and are in fact considered by most who have examined them to have been committed by separate individuals, despite recently released FBI files that conclude that taunting letters mailed to police from Atlanta (postmark of the taunting Aardsma letter) and Williamsport (a short drive from State College) in the 1980s "cannot be ruled out" as potential Zodiac letters.

Gareth Penn, a researcher who has written a number of works about the Zodiac Killer, and who has even been accused of being the Zodiac Killer in some circles because of his detailed theories on how and why the Zodiac Killer operated, believes that the Aardsma murder is not a Zodiac crime, but merely a coincidence:

> "As to the Aardsma murder, which is new to me, let me point out that there are two kinds of coincidences, the kind that happen spontaneously, and those that happen because somebody made them happen. I suggest that the Aardsma murder belongs in the first category, rather like the death of Thomas Jefferson and John Adams, both of whom died on the Fourth of July 1826, the fiftieth anniversary of the date on

140

which they had both signed the Declaration of Independence. An example of the second kind is the bombing of the federal office building in Oklahoma City on the second anniversary of the Branch Davidian disaster. In addition to being a contrived coincidence, it is another example of nonverbal communication. If Timothy McVeigh had made good his escape, he might have written an anonymous letter to the New York Times explaining that the Oklahoma City bombing was revenge for Waco. But he didn't need to. Plenty of people got the point anyway. All he had to do was light the fuse and let the calendar do his talking for him."

* * *

There exists to this day a somewhat maligned school of thought that the Zodiac killer "evolved" his style from attacks on couples at close range into long range attacks based on principal and intended to strike back at a society that had spurned him – the modus operandi of the Unabomber, Theodore John Kaczynski. Again, with the increasing media attention that the

Aardsma murder received in recent years, the speculation has arisen that the Unabomber may have killed Aardsma, either as the Zodiac Killer or as a precursor to his bombings.

Kaczynski had received his Master's degree as well as his Ph.D. from the University of Michigan, in 1964 and 1967, consecutively – Aardsma had transferred to Ann Arbor in the Fall of 1967. Kaczynski's family was from Lombard, Illinois, near where Betsy's steady boyfriend Wright called home. All of these are fascinating coincidences, perhaps -- but nothing substantial.

In an attempt to dispel the Unabomber suspicions once and for all, I decided to go right to the source. I spoke with David Kaczynski, the Unabomber's brother, in the summer of 2010. A staunch advocate for abolishing the death penalty, David is nevertheless an approachable and easy-going man who admits and understands what his brother did, and has a unique insight into his brother's crimes. I asked David about whether he thought that Ted could have stabbed Aardsma, and he answered:

142

"I've read all of the tens of thousands of pages of his notes and diaries. There's no mention of any murders, stabbings, or crimes of that nature. These were documents that he produced for his own personal use – he never intended for anyone else to read them, and never expected that they would be discovered. But to answer your question, it would really surprise me if Ted had done something like that. Obviously, he's surprised me before, but I'd be very, very surprised if he had done this."

The timeline neither supports nor discourages speculation that Kaczynski could have murdered Aardsma. He resigned from his position at the University of California as a math professor on June 30th, 1969. He and his brother purchased land together in Lincoln, Montana, when Ted began building his cabin. His movements during that time period are largely unaccounted for. However, a 1978 letter that Kaczynski had written to a female co-worker who spurned him, but never delivered, seems to finally put the theory to rest.

In the letter, which he showed to his brother David, he wrote of how the woman had made him feel, and how he wanted to wait for her in her car with a knife, and had in fact done so, hoping to catch her and mutilate her, but that he had second thoughts and the last minute and did not carry through with his plan. This letter, written as an apology intended to be read by the woman, was not delivered by Kaczynski, who later explained to his brother that he "couldn't bring himself to do it."

If Kaczynski had these homicidal thoughts in 1978 but failed to carry through with them, why, then, should we be asked to suspect that Kaczynski could have killed Betsy Aardsma with a knife through the heart in 1969? In asking this question, I also spoke with a psychologist who had written a number of letters to Kaczynski while he was in jail, and had published several articles on the subject. He directed me to a psychological profile of Kaczynski that was produced by the FBI, and it confirmed what I had felt all along -- Kaczynski killed from afar, and did not have the stomach to watch his victims suffer. Whoever killed Betsy had to look into her eyes as she took her last breath, knowing full well what he had done.

Chris's Story

2009 found the Aardsma case at a standstill. There were a number of articles that came out, including the 2009 State College Magazine article that outed Richard Haefner and his strange behavior for the first time. Several newspapers in the local area also did "40th anniversary" stories, but for the most part there seemed to be little else that could be done to push the case forward. In 2009, Trooper Kent Bernier, who had been assigned to the Aardsma case since 2005, was reassigned, and his replacement, Trooper Leigh Ann Barrows, took over control of the case at Rockview.

In the Pennsylvania State Police, at least at Rockview, cold cases like the Aardsma murder come with the desk. The individual who is investigating them passes them down to the next person to take their spot, while the cold case assistance officer at the Hollidaysburg barracks remains as their partner on the case. Because of the fact that the cold case officer has a number of different charges, the individual Trooper remains in charge of the investigation, and is given control over the decisions that are made in the case. Of

145

course, it is always better if the Trooper in charge of the investigation has the cooperation and support of the cold case officer, so that they are working together with the same suspects in mind.

The theory in investigating individuals related to the Aardsma case has always been to look for information that could clear them; to find a reason that they couldn't have done it. Robert Durgy, for example, was cleared easily once it came out that he had left the University with his family the day before the murder. The same was true for Ted Bundy – once he could definitively be placed somewhere else, we could rule out his involvement. It was with this mindset that I decided to look into Rick Haefner – surely, his showing up at Wright's house could have been a coincidence, and someone could have the crucial piece of evidence that would place him somewhere else that day and allow everyone to concentrate on finding the real killer.

It might seem like researching an individual who had been deceased for several years would be a fairly straightforward task. This quickly proved not to be the case for Rick Haefner. He seemed to have very few friends while he was alive, and some of the people he knew didn't want to talk about him. His entire family was deceased – his father in 1983, his mother in 1991, and his brother and sister-in-law in 2009 and 2010. Rick had no children of his own, and his two nephews were younger, and from the West Coast, and likely had little contact with Rick before he died.

I decided to try to find someone who might have known him by posting on genealogy forums and Craigslist. At the beginning of February, 2010, within days of posting an advertisement asking for anyone who might have known Rick Haefner, I received a response from Chris Haefner, a cousin of Rick, who was in his mid-fifties and had worked with Rick at his rock-cracking operation in Lancaster in the 1970s. Chris was "the best rock-cracker Rick ever had," by his own accounts, and had worked with Rick on and off from about 1973-74 through the early 1990s, when Chris would help with the Lost Dutchman Gemboree shows Rick put on for gem and mineral collectors.

Chris was related to Rick through a strange family tree. He called himself Rick's "nousin," because he was technically a nephew, but was more like a cousin. The Haefner family tree was convoluted – two brothers had married two sisters, and Chris's father was Rick's father's brother, while his mother was Rick's mother's sister. His father was younger than Rick's parents, and consequently Chris and his brother had grown up around Rick, but were much younger than he was and so had not had too much experience with them, except for the fact that Chris had worked for Rick.

The initial email account of the story Chris told went like this:

> What happened that day in the rock shop was very intense, very detailed. My aunt didn't know I was there the way the shop was configured - you would have to see it. She approached it from outside the swung-open doors. Later, after the incident, Rick went back inside the house which was 10-feet away and they argued intensely again, this time about the fact that what had happened, happened in front of me. This time Rick was pissed. I was the only other person there.
>
> I don't remember all the words but I clearly remember the crux of them. They implicated him for killing 'THAT GIRL' from Penn State. Aunt Ere

148

firmly accused him in a way that said he had told her and she forgave him, protected him. Rick never moved out of his mom's house, never married, never had children. If the people at Penn State ever knew about Rick's later life, all the things he did, they would have thoroughly investigated him. If my word isn't good enough then, whatever! It's their loss. I am not being a judge or jury here. I am relating pertinent information about a young girl's death from something that took place many years ago. Remember, I never knew about Betsy or this case before February 8, 2010. That's all. I have told the truth. the whole truth. and nothing but the truth - so help me God!

Essentially, in the late summer of 1975, Rick had been arrested and charged with molesting two young neighborhood boys who worked with him. Although Chris couldn't recall the exact date, the exchange that he was talking about must have taken place shortly after police interviewed him on August 15th, 1975. As Chris told it, he had been cracking rocks and helping to prepare rock boxes in the garage across the street from Rick's home where he lived with his parents. Rick's mother, Ere Haefner, had come out of the home and, not realizing that Chris was at work in the garage, cornered Rick outside and began berating him about getting in trouble again after all she had done for him to help him get out of trouble.

At the climax of the argument, Ere screamed at Rick:

"You killed that girl, and now you're killing me."

Rick was alternately arguing with her and trying to calm her down, and finally she looked at him and said: "Are you going to kill me too Rick?" She threw up her hands and went back into the house. Rick stewed for a few minutes, then followed her back inside. The windows were open in the August heat, and Chris could clearly hear Rick chastising his mother for having that conversation out there – where Chris could overhear it. He came back out a few moments later and they continued working on rock cracking and processing the rock boxes. Nothing further was said about what had happened.

Chris's story was compelling. Along with his story of the rock shop incident, Chris expanded on his knowledge of Rick with a few other pieces of information that we were able to corroborate and begin investigating. Previous to returning to Lancaster, in 1975, Rick had worked as a professor at the University of Charleston in South Carolina for a year, then had worked at the State University of New York in New Paltz, teaching classes in geology. He had returned to Lancaster and continued working on the rock shop, which brought in a considerable income – they would pack a few thousand rock boxes per year and sell them for $3-$5 each to the Smithsonian gift shop in Washington, DC. This job, and some money won during a lawsuit, would be Rick's sole source of income until he started the Lost Dutchman Gemboree in the 1980s.

Chris also mentioned Rick's almost pathological need to "explain" things to people. He was often getting in trouble, and would take Chris up to Penn State with him to meet with his former professors, where the conversation would usually begin with: "Have you seen the papers?" Followed by Rick's convoluted and mostly untrue explanations of why he had been falsely accused of this, or wrongfully charged with that. This would prove interesting, because it explained some of his behavior at Wright's house on the night of the murder – a potential attempt to gain an ally and stave off suspicion when the headlines about the murder broke. It also fit with the man who, after stabbing Betsy Aardsma through the heart, would stop to tell a bystander that "That girl needs help," leading her to the body before finally making his escape.

In recalling Rick and his experiences with him, Chris also provided an insight into Rick's character and personal life. Chris had always believed that Rick was gay, and knew that he was a pedophile. Indeed, he had been warned by other family members to "be careful around Rick." Chris knew the names of some other boys who had worked for Rick, and who may have been molested or sexually involved with Rick.

Chris never saw any women visit Rick, and never recalled Rick expressing interest in females – only young boys. He also gave us insight into Rick's predatory style of recruiting young boys under his employ. Rick was fond of "feeling out" the proclivities of the boys who worked for him, slowly working on them, taking them on field trips, and making them feel special. Once he felt he could safely make advances, he would move forward

– but he was smart enough to know which boys would succumb to his advances and which would resist.

According to Chris, the boys who accused Rick of molesting them in 1975 had not actually been molested – Rick had approached them and they had told their parents, setting off an outrage. In his mind, this explained why Rick had passed a polygraph test when police accused him of molesting the boys.

Chris had also been one of the last people to view Rick's things after his death. In 2006, George Haefner, Rick's brother, had offered to sell the house at Nevin Street to Chris's side of the family. He and his brother and father had cleaned out the home in 2006, in preparation for selling it. All of the contents of the home – Rick's files, his computer, and most everything else, went into the dumpster. Thus, the chance at finding any physical evidence or written records at the Haefner home likely ended in 2006, before police were even aware of his involvement.

Rick Haefner, 1965-1972

Richard Charles Haefner was born on December
13th, 1943, to his parents, George Haefner and Ere J.
Haefner, nee Seaber. As a young man, Rick attended
Lancaster Catholic High School, while his father worked
as a fire marshal and his mother looked after Rick and
his older brother George. Despite their generally
mundane occupations – Ere was a housewife and
George was functionally retired except for his work in the
rock shop -- Ere used what money they had to help her
sons succeed at life – education being key to their
success in her eyes.

George was a 1965 graduate of Penn State, and
had gone on to become a successful electrical engineer,
working for the United States Space Program in
California, when Rick graduated high school. Rick, the
introspective young man with the Eddie Haskell grin who
had always been quiet and reserved, had been
interested in rocks and minerals ever since middle
school. He had a knack for finding excellent specimens
of rare and valuable minerals, and for identifying them
easily. Something about working with rocks was

attractive to Rick, and he quickly made a name for himself as a go-to guy in the local mineralogy circles.

When it was time to attend college, it made sense that Rick would pick Franklin and Marshall College. Besides being located only a few miles from the family home on Nevin Street in Lancaster, Franklin and Marshall had an excellent reputation and a long history. The college had been founded in 1787 by Benjamin Franklin under the name Franklin College, and a nearby college in Mercersburg had been incorporated by a Supreme Court Justice, John J. Marshall, in 1827. In 1853, the colleges merged, becoming Franklin & Marshall College and keeping the Lancaster campus as their operational center.

Franklin and Marshall had the dual benefits of being a local college with an excellent reputation, and having a museum on the campus, where Rick had started volunteering during his senior year in high school, when he tested out of Lancaster Catholic and took college classes instead. The North Museum at Franklin and Marshall College was a veritable "Lancaster Smithsonian," which was overseen by the college and which contained thousands of artifacts of all kinds that related to Lancaster's history.

Even before his F&M years, he worked at the family business, with the help of his father, where the pair would collect gems and minerals and crack them into smaller samples, after which they would glue the samples onto labeled cards and place them into specimen boxes. Each collection – and the number of collections varied, from "Local Minerals of Lancaster County," to larger collections that came later and were destined for sale to the Smithsonian and other museums – would be taken to local tourist traps and sold as souvenirs. Rick could always count on his father's help while he was at college, and the extra money the business provided was welcome. Thankfully, Rick could also count on his doting, domineering mother and his shrinking violet father to manage the money that he made from his rock kits.

Rick was known as socially awkward and a bit quiet. Most students from the F&M years who had any recollection of him at all remembered him as quiet, well-dressed, soft-spoken, and self-possessed. He stayed to himself, and while knowledgeable, was not always easy to get along with, or easy to get close to. He preferred to work by himself. R.G. Hirnisey, who performed a quadrant study with Rick while they were undergraduates at F&M, said "He really had no hint of violence in him at the time. He was quiet and well-mannered." Angelo Okuma, another F&M classmate, had similar recollections of Rick.

During the years that Rick attended Franklin and Marshall, the college was not a coeducational facility. Outside of the wives of current students and a few select others, women would not be admitted to Franklin and Marshall openly until 1969. Very few opportunities existed for Rick to meet members of the opposite sex, and he likely didn't date very much. This may have suited him. Rick seemed more interested in some of the young boys who came around the neighborhood, and if he wasn't volunteering with the local Boy Scouts, he was taking the boys into the North Museum and showing off his vast knowledge of gems and minerals, or taking them on field trips to show off historic geological sites in Lancaster like the Cedar Hill Quarry or the Pequea Silver Mines.

The work at the North Museum was really where Rick excelled, however. Former professors and curators recalled that Rick was the man who you would want to see walking past if you were having trouble identifying a rock or mineral specimen. All he had to do was pop his head in the door, take a look at what you were stumped by, and he would rattle off, from memory, the scientific name and classification of the rock or mineral. It didn't matter what it was -- if it came from the ground, Rick knew all about it. He was a valuable person to have around.

Rick had also had the honor of discovering a mineral in Lancaster in 1965, along with a friend of his, Jerry Lintner. The two had discovered a mineral they called Haefnerite, but because Rick had not dedicated much time to officially classifying and registering his discovery, he would be trumped by a team of scientists halfway around the world, who discovered the same mineral in Japan. To history, Haefnerite ended up as nakauriite - and Rick missed his chance to get his name into the mineral history books.

Whether he was angry about this or not, it was his own fault for not registering the mineral sooner, and herein lay one of the fundamental paradoxes that would repeat itself throughout Rick's life. He was knowledgeable, skilled, and book-smart, but he was often unmotivated and misguided. He would spend his time in pursuits that would not benefit him or would even prove detrimental, and he seemed almost incapable of redirecting himself from these dalliances.

During his time at the North Museum, Rick had produced a number of pamphlets on local geological history, such as one titled "Historic Mines of Lancaster County," which had been checked for accuracy by Dr. John Price of the Museum. Rick was already on his way to becoming a published, lettered geologist, but his failure to secure his place in the geological lexicon with Haefnerite was merely the beginning of problematic behavior that would cause him to have to disassociate from the North Museum.

One of the first rumblings of trouble came from the disappearance of a number of specimens from the North Museum. Rick worked obsessively and was there almost every day, yet valuable and rare specimens continued to disappear. When asked, Rick had no answer for the shrinkage of the museum's collection. He was unable to account for the fact that the collection was literally being pillaged under his care. There were other problems, too – disturbing letters and reports from parents that the brown-haired, knowledgeable young caretaker at the museum had attempted to touch or fondle their sons when they visited the exhibits. Rick always seemed to try to get the boys alone, and several of them had told their parents that they felt uncomfortable in his presence. A few letters to the men in charge of the North Museum were enough to get Rick disciplined officially. W. Fred Kinsey was one of these men.

Kinsey recalled that Rick had been asked to leave the North Museum because of the reports, and in order to help avoid a problem for Rick down the line, the reasons were listed as a difference of opinion. "So I'm not allowed to come down here anymore, is that what you're telling me?" Rick seemed oblivious to the fact that he was getting off easy – local parents wanted him in trouble, and he was being shown the exit politely rather than being carried there. "I can't tell you not to come here anymore," Kinsey replied. He was disassociating the Museum from Rick Haefner, but he couldn't prohibit a grown man from stopping by.

Rick had powerful allies at the Museum as well. Dr. John Price, a retired volunteer firefighter and fossil collector who had been so helpful and so devoted to the North Museum and its activities and collections that he had been awarded a number of honorary titles by the college, among them a Doctorate, was a particularly good friend of Rick's. Besides his affiliation with the Haefner family through his father George, the fire marshal, Dr. Price had grown up as an orphan and had become a local guru of rocks and minerals, and he saw something in the young Haefner, whether it was the gleam in his eye or the knowledge that he brought to the table, that made him take Rick under his wing. For years following his exit from the North Museum under dubious circumstances, Rick would continue to come back to visit with "Doc" Price whenever he was in the area.

In the fall of 1965, Rick enrolled at Penn State University, in the challenging Geology program, with the goal of getting his Master's degree. He was an average student, pulling a 3.29 career GPA in a program that normally chewed up and spit out students who couldn't keep pace. Rick seemed to be able to hold his own, despite producing fieldwork results that were described variously by his professors as "sloppy" and "mediocre." He wasn't the top of his class, but he had knowledge and skills. These skills resulted in him receiving a key and administrative privileges to the Deike Museum of Mineral Sciences, a combination museum and mineralogy library located in the Deike Building of the Penn State campus that is open to students and the public. One former acquaintance would report hearing that Rick would occasionally sleep in the library there.

Many of Rick's fellow classmates from the Penn State years had as little to say about him as his F&M classmates. Again, out of dozens of classmates who were asked to recall what they could about Rick Haefner, only a few had any memories whatsoever. One female classmate remembered "sleeping in the front seat of a car while Rick slept in the back" on field trips, and recalled that, while she was attractive, Rick never seemed to be the least bit interested in her, and unlike most of the other young men in the geology department, he never attempted to hit on her or otherwise make a move. "He was, in that respect, a perfect gentleman," she recalled.

There were strange undercurrents, however. Specimens had begun disappearing from the Deike Building, and the female classmate who recalled Rick as "the perfect gentleman" remembers that his behavior was, at times, strange. A few months after the murder of Aardsma, as they sat on the lawn eating lunch one day, Rick opened up, telling his classmate that "I knew that girl who got murdered in the library. I used to date her." She replied "Oh no! That must be hard for you! What a horrible thing to have to go through!" To which Rick answered only with a blank stare and stony silence. No emotion, no connection to his alleged former girlfriend.

Other professors who knew him, both from F&M and Penn State, remembered an average student – nothing outstanding about him, just average. Professors weren't the only ones who noticed his lackadaisical attention to detail. One classmate, who worked with Rick assisting with fieldwork for his thesis, remembered him being "sloppy" and "incomplete." Sharp when he wanted to be, but sloppy and even lazy on many occasions, Haefner somehow managed to continue to thrive in the fast-paced, highly competitive Penn State geosciences department.

Rick had trouble keeping roommates, as well. Having changed rooms, at least on paper, three times in the fall of 1969, he had also ended up across from Betsy's floor. She was in the basement of Atherton Hall, while Rick was in room 64, by himself – he had noticed that a Greek student who had graduated in August of 1969 had left the room empty, and he put in for a transfer. Previously, he had occupied Room 48 with another student – who still lives with his aging mother in Florida, and who quickly told me in 2010 that he had "no recollection" of Rick Haefner, before hanging up the phone. From his place in room 64, Rick could have seen the lights in Betsy's room at night, across the courtyard at the center of Atherton Hall.

Although he had begun to form a reputation as an aloof and distant classmate, Haefner had an uncanny ability to endear himself to some of his professors. One of these, paleontology professor Roger Cuffey, was especially fond of Rick. Cuffey is a man with a booming, radio announcer voice, who came to Penn State in 1967 after serving as a Captain in the Army in Vietnam. Rick was his teaching assistant from 1967-1970, and Cuffey recalled that Rick was "an outgoing, excellent student; his work was well done, and he was friendly to everyone he met."

Cuffey remembered Rick standing outside of the lecture hall before classes, greeting other young men and women as they walked into class. "He was the opposite of a homosexual, from what I could see. I knew men in Vietnam who were closeted gays, and Rick didn't come across like them at all." He was shocked when I spoke with him and suggested that Rick may have been involved in the Aardsma murder.

But even Cuffey had seen a strange side of Rick – the earliest signs of trouble in the young man's otherwise composed exterior. Rick had come to him in 1967 with a problem. Cuffey was not surprised – as a Captain in Vietnam, he had often counseled young men under his command. Rick asked to speak with him, and in his characteristic rambling fashion, began to explain what was on his mind. According to Cuffey, Rick stated that he was having problems in Lancaster. "Powerful men" from Lancaster and Philadelphia were "conspiring against him," charging him with child molestation and forcing him out of his work at the North Museum. Rick told Cuffey that he had "contacted a young Philadelphia District Attorney, Arlen Specter," who had looked into the allegations, chose to believe Rick, and "made the charges go away." Cuffey chose to believe his young teaching assistant, and does to this day. He remains impressed with Specter for "going to bat for this young man."

While the story may have been far-fetched, there was a kernel of truth to it, as there almost always was with Rick's stories. He HAD been accused of child molestation and booted from the North Museum, but that's where the similarities end. There had never been

165

any formal charges, and there was no reason to think that Specter had "gone to bat for him." The Museum had severed ties with Haefner and asked him politely to stay away. That was Rick, though – always explaining himself in advance of any potential bad press or rumors that might make their way to those he respected and considered his superiors. Phone calls and emails to now-Senator Arlen Specter's office, asking if he recalled Haefner or if any of the story might have been true went unreturned, but someone from the Congressional offices visited the Whokilledbetsy.org site, according to the internet logs.

Rick was under intense pressure from his mother during this period to curb his homosexual inclinations, which she was aware of. Apparently, Rick had been caught by Ere *in flagrante delicto* with a neighborhood boy while in high school. Certainly, she had scolded him, explaining that those types of behaviors were not compatible with a professional, with a Ph.D. student, with an intelligent boy like her son. A friend of Rick's from F&M and up until the early 1970s remembers Rick bragging one night at dinner about the girl he was dating at Penn State. He also spoke about Rick explaining to his mother that he wanted to spend Thanksgiving at

Penn State that year – odd, considering Lancaster is only a short hour to hour and a half drive from the University, and he could easily have come home.

Aside from his relationship with Betsy as reported to the State Police, Rick's dating life was as nonexistent at Penn State as it had been at Franklin and Marshall, despite the fact that Penn State was a coeducational facility that offered a wide range of women who would have been pleased to meet such an eligible suitor. The memories of Rick held by his classmates and professors are similar to those held by his colleagues at the North Museum: he would bring young boys from Lancaster up to take tours of the campus, taking them to Pattee Library and into the stacks, as well as to the Deike Library of Earth and Mineral Sciences. The boys were Scouts or youth group members, he told his friends.

Some of these boys were his employees at the rock shop, or his assistants with his graduate studies. One of the boys recalled being taken up to Pattee Library in the spring or summer of 1970, at the age of fifteen. Rick told him to follow him down into the stacks, and he stopped at one point, instructing the boy to go down a particular aisle. "Stop right there," Rick said. "Stand still, and be quiet." The boy thought Rick was going to ask him to look for a book, or for some other type of assistance. "A girl that I used to date was murdered here." He paused. "You're standing in the exact spot where it happened." After telling him this, Rick motioned for him to come out of the aisle, and they went on about their business.

"He was completely emotionless when he said this to me," the man later recalled. "It wasn't like he was trying to scare me; he wasn't joking. He was very matter-of-fact about it."

Despite his odd and at some times inscrutable behavior, Something about Rick had endeared him to one of his instructors, Dr. Lauren Wright, and the two became close, with Rick's area of expertise becoming volcanology, and his interests beginning to mirror those of Wright, who spent most of his time in Death Valley, California, studying volcanic formations. Rick would become a protégé of Wright, perhaps second to none, and he and Wright would remain lifelong friends.

Lauren Wright is another professor who has achieved much in life. One could say he is the geological equivalent of Harrison Meserole, Betsy's English 501 professor. Wright, formerly of the California Division of Mines and Geology, had by 1969 already written a number of definitive guides and studies of the Death Valley area. He had worked with famed petrologists such as C. Wayne Burnham and Bennie Troxel to create groundbreaking understanding of the Death Valley area, and he had returned to Penn State to continue that work and to pass his knowledge on to the next generation of geology students.

Wright was known among his colleagues as a man who never had a bad word to say about anyone, and who always tried to find the best in people, he was known to many of his students as a fearsome instructor. Often called by the nicknames "Mostly Wright" or "Seldom Wright," depending on the opinion they had of him, student advisors sometimes counseled new members of the geology program to avoid Wright at all costs, to try not to take any problems or questions to him, and generally to keep things very professional and very civil, lest they rouse his ire. Several students from the department recalled never being able to get on the same page as Wright, and feeling that, while he was a good instructor, he operated on a different wavelength than they did, both personally and professionally.

Rick Haefner never seemed to have these problems, at least as far as others could tell. He often assisted Wright with his fieldwork in Death Valley, and in fact Rick's Masters and Doctoral Thesis publications were both on the igneous petrology of lava flows in the Death Valley area. Haefner seemed to be Lauren Wright's chosen disciple, and he spent much of his college career viewing Wright as a sort of mentor, father figure, and friend.

This may explain why he showed up at Wright's doorstep the night of Betsy Aardsma's murder, out of breath and desperate to share the knowledge of his ex-girlfriend's death with someone he knew and trusted. This may also explain Wright's hesitation in pursuing the idea of reporting Rick to the authorities at the time. Why ruin Rick's life, and why assume anything other than the fact that his young colleague was upset about the untimely death of a former flame?

In 1975 or 1976, about the time that Richard Haefner was being investigated for involuntary deviate sexual intercourse, Lauren Wright finally met with the Dean of the Mineral Sciences department, Charlie Hosler, to tell him about his experience on the night of the Aardsma murder a few years before. In Hosler's office, he told the Dean about his strange visit from

170

Richard Haefner. Hosler and his assistant, Alex Martin[4], listened to the story and when Wright was finished, Hosler said that they should report it.

He told Wright that he would pass the information along to the University attorney, Delbert J. McQuaide. They did, but apparently nothing further was ever done with that information. McQuaide apparently never mentioned the information to police – at least, if he did, there is no record of it in the police files. Wright and Hosler, apparently never forced the issue, and Martin did not either. They assumed, perhaps, that they had done their duty, and when they heard nothing more from McQuaide or the police, that Haefner had been cleared and was not a suspect.

Sadly, McQuaide never relayed his findings or his work to anyone else, either. He died in 1997, taking his knowledge of the Haefner incident to his grave. His former partner, Attorney John Blasko, remembered only that his friend had worked for Penn State for many years, and his widow was equally uninformed.

"Delbert never brought his work home," his widow Barbara told me pleasantly on a phone call from North Carolina. "In fact, I have only a vague recollection

---

[4]   Name has been changed.

of reading articles about the case. He never mentioned anything about it to me."

Whether or not Wright was familiar with Rick's idiosyncrasies, this familiarity with Rick does not explain another story about Rick's misdeeds that had occurred a year prior to the Aardsma murder and that Wright had become aware of in the Spring of 1968. During the fall or winter semester of 1967, Rick and Lauren had been out in the Death Valley area, working on research. Rick had been introduced to a young woman out there named Mary Kelling[5], who was distantly related to a former California Senator.

Mary was a vivacious, free-spirited girl, much like Betsy Aardsma. A few years younger than Rick, she went to college in the east, at Brown University in Massachusetts, and she was home on break. She wanted to join the Peace Corps in Africa after she graduated college, and indeed she would, serving in Liberia in 1973. She was about 5'8" tall, with curly brown hair worn in a hippy style, and she was attractive. She noticed Rick leering at her that fall, and was sure that he was interested in her. He would try to make small talk, and she would try to avoid it. Her mother

---

[5]   Name has been changed.

172

joked openly that she would "hook Rick up with her daughter," and Rick must have hoped against hope that this would be true.

Mary was relieved that she would no longer have to see Rick when she returned to Brown for the Spring semester in 1968. Her relief turned to fear, however, with a knock on her door one day that spring. Opening it, she found Rick Haefner standing outside her dorm room, unannounced, and almost unable to contain his excitement. "What are you doing here?" She asked, to which Rick replied that he was in love with her, and that he wanted to be with her and had come to surprise her – that he had come 800 miles away from his home, unannounced, to surprise a woman he barely knew.

Kelling was deeply unsettled, as much by the unannounced visit as by the demeanor of the visitor, and she told Rick that he would have to leave, immediately, and not to contact her again or she would tell the police. She recalled that his expression changed almost instantly, that he became "like a sad puppy dog," and that he left her dorm. A few days later, after retelling the story to her friends, they recalled that a strange man fitting Rick's description had been lingering around campus, asking about her and where she roomed. Mary told her mother, who was a personal friend of Lauren Wright, and her mother told Wright, asking that he do something about his students, especially Haefner, to prevent this sort of thing from happening again. If Wright did anything, it certainly wasn't much, as Rick remained in the program and no official record exists of any kind of disciplinary action.

This account is the earliest record of Rick showing an interest in a female, and the method by which he chose to do it is telling. It shows an almost total lack of understanding on Rick's part of how women operate, and what appropriate means of communicating with and approaching young women romantically involves.

The incident also shows a strange side of Rick – that he would think that this young woman, who had openly tried to avoid him in Shoshone, might be not only receptive to his advances but excited to see that he had "dropped in" to her dorm, and might even reciprocate his feelings. The bold declaration that he was in love with her, that he "wanted her," is even stranger.

Wright knew about this incident, and likely may have known about Rick's alleged dates with Betsy, in 1969, and nothing happened. The police were never made aware of what Wright and Hosler had told the University attorney, and as a result, Richard Haefner would be virtually ignored as a suspect in the Aardsma murder.

There are hints, however, that Rick was investigated more closely than the surviving police records might indicate; and there are disturbing allegations that his mother may have lied in order to keep him out of trouble. Whatever the case, the mild-mannered, quiet, well-dressed Rick Haefner would begin to change after the Aardsma murder, becoming a wild, uncontrolled, violent man prone to outbursts and vindictive behavior. Rick after 1969 is almost a completely different man.

According to one source, a boy who worked for Rick in his rock shop in 1970, there was further collusion between Rick and his family around the time of the Aardsma murder. One day, after having been taken to the library by Rick and being asked to stand in the spot where Aardsma had been murdered, he had been eating his lunch inside the kitchen of the home at Nevin Street with Ere. Curious about what Rick had subjected him to, he asked her what had happened at Penn State. Seemingly unconcerned, Ere replied: "Oh yes, the police asked me where Rick was that night. He was up there, but I told them that he was here with us. I lied to keep him out of jail." She seemed upset with the fact that Rick had asked this of her – lying to police.

It's unclear who came to visit the Haefner residence to confirm Rick's whereabouts the night of the murder. If it was the PA State Police at Rockview, it should be in the case file. There does not appear to be any reference to this incident in the file, and none of the retired officers were aware of it. Perhaps the notes were lost, or perhaps one of the investigators had "called in a favor," asking a Trooper from the Lancaster area to check in, or even simply made a phone call and did not bother to write it down. Rick's story had checked out, and his own mother had covered for him, as she would do for him later on. The Lancaster Troop of the Pennsylvania State Police have no record of interviewing Haefner's mother.

Regardless of why he was able to escape further scrutiny from the police and his colleagues in 1969, it is easy to see how Rick could have avoided suspicion in the Aardsma murder after December, 1969. Besides the fact that police would release Marilee Erdley's sketch of the killer, which looks like almost any college student attending Penn State at the time, instead of the sketch made from Uafinda and the desk clerk's description – a sketch that is a spitting image of Rick -- a quick look at his schedule shows that he would spend the next two years studying almost exclusively off campus, or working on research outside of the traditional class structure.

A large portion of the later part of an advanced geology degree at Penn State in those years was the GEO 600 series of classes – Essentially independent studies, where the student did not have to attend any classes, but would instead work on independent research or assist their advisor with their research. Rick would spend very little time on campus after the Aardsma murder and before his graduation in 1972 with a Ph.D. in Geology.

Richard Haefner, 1972-1986

Despite his knowledge of the subject matter, Haefner struggled academically – having trouble adhering to deadlines and regulations. In fact, Haefner barely received his Ph.D. at Penn State in 1972. His usual procrastination and disorganization had worked against him yet again. Thesis documents are due at least a week in advance of the defense part of the thesis presentation, and Rick had handed his in the day of his thesis defense. The men who signed off on his Doctoral thesis had to discuss among themselves whether to accept it or not. They did, and Rick was able to defend his thesis and graduate from Penn State. After graduation, Rick took the route of many young Ph.D. students, applying for and accepting a number of different teaching jobs, travelling to various parts of the country to instruct.

In 1972, Rick took a job teaching geology as a visiting professor at the State University of New York, New Paltz campus. While there, he continued his "charity work" with young boys. A former colleague from SUNY remembered his shock one night when he visited a restaurant in town and found Rick eating dinner along with a boy who must have been around ten years old. Rick explained it away – "He is a Boy Scout and I'm working with his troop," he said. The only other impression of Rick that his supervisors could remember was that he hated smoking, and had once gone into a tirade on a plane when a man in the seat next to him lit a cigarette while he and his supervisor were traveling somewhere.

Rick was not asked to renew his contract with SUNY. His former supervisor remembered vaguely that he had gone against University policy in the summer of 1972 by choosing to spend the summer boating on the Finger Lakes in New York, rather than working on research in his field, which was the approved and preferred summer activity for assistant professors who wished to eventually receive tenure track positions there. It didn't matter much to Rick – he still had the rock shop, and his father continued to work there in his absence, earning him money and keeping the contracts they had with the Smithsonian, as well as the various local museums and gift shops, alive.

According to his own curriculum vitae, Rick worked at the University of Charleston in South Carolina from 1973 to 1974. No one from the University was able to confirm or deny that he had worked there, and no one in the geology department had any recollection of the former assistant professor. After one year at the University of Charleston, Rick quit the job there for unknown reasons and returned home, jobless, to help out with the rock shop. In 1975, he would receive a job offer that would change his life.

Marion Stuart, the heiress to the Carnation Milk fortune and a devoted gem and mineral collector, had taken notice to Rick through his application for the position of Curator at the LA Museum of Natural History and his attendance at the Tucson Gem Show, held each year during the first two weeks of February in Tucson, Arizona. The Tucson show is the largest gem and mineral show in the country, and is known among rockhounds as a "must see" event.

Using her fortune, Stuart had created an endowed position at the University of Southern California, Los Angeles, which was given to along with the curatorship at the Los Angeles Museum of Natural History. She had chosen Rick as the most qualified candidate for the position, and his future was clearly defined. He would assume the prestigious position after a formal announcement at a dinner in Tucson in early 1976.

Elated by his success, and having at the age of 32 obtained one of the most prestigious positions in the field of geology, Rick quit his job at the University of Charleston, renounced any other outstanding job offers, and returned home to Nevin Street in the summer of 1975 to work at his rock shop and await the 1976 Tucson Gem and Mineral Show, where he would give a speech and his acceptance of the position would formally be announced.

Rick's world came crashing down around him in August 15th, 1975, with his arrest on charges of corrupting the morals of a minor and sodomizing a child. Two boys who had worked in Rick's rock shop, Kevin Burkey and Randy Klivansky, had told their parents about alleged advances Rick had made against them on July 3rd, 1975. Police came to visit him on August 15th, taking him into custody on the charges. Rick consented to and, in the opinion of the examining officer, passed a polygraph test at the police station, and although he was quickly freed on bail, things quickly turned from bad to worse for Rick once the proceedings started.

Evidence came out at trial that Rick had employed a 17 year old boy, Steven Groff, along with some other boys, to take the young Burkey boy on a series of car rides where they interrogated him about what had happened and why he was making these accusations. During the rides, in which Burkey was presumably intimidated by the older boys, the interrogators illegally recorded the conversations, providing them to Rick, who had them transcribed before giving them to his attorney.

Other family friends, like Terry Hess, an employee of a local appliance store, testified that they had seen police officer Jerry Crump bribing one of the boys in the men's room during the trial, telling him "You know what you have to do, now go out there and say it." Hess, who refused to waiver from his story, would later be charged with perjury.

During the trial, the transcripts and recordings of the illegal car rides disappeared, and Groff was threatened with a wiretapping charge by the Lancaster District Attorney's Office. Rick blurted out that he had passed a lie detector test – evidence that had been deemed inadmissible in court, and was charged with contempt, for which he paid a $500 fine and spent two weeks in jail.

* * *

"I always thought he was strange, but I never figured him for a cocksucker!" Rick's friend and former mentor, John Price, told Jim McMullen, one of the Lancaster County Police Cadets who had been working the night Rick was arrested, and a personal friend to Price. Rick was one of Price's "boys," a group of young science aficionados known as "The Explorers," who met at the North Museum and learned about geology and paleontology from the knowledgeable, friendly Dr. Price.

Dr. Price, who had known Rick since high school, and who believed Rick's theory that he was being persecuted, pushed hard for his friend McMullen to convince police to drop the charges and for him to talk some sense into Jerry Crump, the arresting officer. The disagreement between Price and McMullen over the nature and scope of Rick's crimes caused a rift between the friends that took many months to heal.

The aging Dr. John Price, who by this point was dying of cancer and was afraid that he would not live to see his young friend exonerated on what he believed were false charges, wound up taking the stand as a character witness to testify on Rick's behalf during the trial. A number of other prominent scientists and educators, as well as a few local boys and former employees of the Haefner family, also served as character witnesses.

Cadet McMullen believed that his fellow officers were mostly correct. According to a number of former officers, the Lancaster City Police and the Lancaster District Attorney's Office had a file on Rick dating back to 1962, alleging indecent conduct and improper contact with young boys. One of Rick's first employers, a manager for the Lancaster Recreation Department, had reported his initial concerns about Rick's strange interest in children after Rick worked for them at the age of 19.

After a prolonged trial, which ended in a hung jury, Rick was released from the charges. According to one of the members of the jury that had resulted in Rick's release on the charges, eleven of the members of the jury were convinced of Rick's guilt. One juror, however, had a hatred of the police in general, and didn't trust the story that the local cops were selling to the court. He refused to vote "guilty," and the proceedings gridlocked, resulting in Rick's release.

Unfortunately for Rick, the damage was already done. He had missed his meeting in Tucson while he was in the Lancaster County Prison on the contempt charges, and Marion Stuart had found out through the grapevine that Rick had been accused of crimes against children and morals offenses. She saw to it that the offer of employment was rescinded. The position would come up again several times throughout the following years, along with a second position as Chief Curator of Earth Sciences, which Rick applied for in 1979. These were high-level positions and suitable candidates were not easily found. Rick continued to apply, and be denied, and finally some of the museum administrators told him flat out why they felt he was unsuitable.

Rick responded with a lawsuit in Los Angeles County against the Museum, the county, and the men who had "discriminated" against him. In 1982, he began collecting the signatures and depositions of individuals who he knew and who he felt might be able to help him. Rick travelled around the country with George and Ere in tow -- collecting depositions, filing briefs, and acting as his own attorney in the matter. He asked for $2.5 million in damages, along with court costs and attorney fees, alleging that he had applied for "over 100 positions since February of 1976" and that the Museum members, by spreading rumors about what he had done and why he had been rejected, had "effectively foreclosed (him) from pursuing any meaningful career in the field of geology."

In 1983, Rick's father George died in an automobile accident a few days after Christmas, leaving him living alone on Nevin Street with his mother. He occasionally flew out to Shoshone, where he had a mining claim with the US Bureau of Land Management. BLM records show that his brother George would file the necessary paperwork for each year, stating that he had done the required amount of improvements to the claim to keep it valid, but it appears that Rick did not spend much time working the claim, and it is unclear exactly what type of minerals Rick was searching for.

The court case would drag on, and would finally be partly upheld and partly struck down. Rick would receive $186,000 in damages, upheld by the 9th District Circuit Court in 1986. This was equivalent to about $475,000 in 2010 dollars. It was a large settlement, but not what Rick had hoped for, and the loss of his father's assistance, along with the public nature of what he had been through, had destroyed his rock shop business as well as his job prospects in the close-knit geology field. While he now had money to support himself even though he wasn't working, it couldn't last forever, especially not with the debts he owed for the various court cases that he had engaged in after the molestation trial ended.

Rick would spend the rest of the 1980s attempting to expunge his record. After a number of attorney changes, as well as lawsuits against his former attorneys, the boys who had accused him, and the police who had arrested him, Rick was successful in getting his record expunged in 1981. Very little information exists about Rick's trial, because expungement completely removes all proceedings of a criminal arrest and hearing from law enforcement agency records. However, through Rick's incessant and vindictive lawsuits, much of what he had sought to cover up became public record in the end, showing up in various court documents and cases later in the 1980s.

One of the few primary documents produced in Rick's own words is a statement Rick gave to FBI investigators at his home in 1982, where he alleged civil rights violations against the Lancaster Police and asked the FBI to open an investigation into corruption in the police department.

According to the FBI, in 1980 Rick had made his way to the Washington Field Office via the office of Senator Barry Goldwater, where he had appeared alleging that his civil rights had been violated, telling them that the "entire Lancaster county justice system was corrupt." Goldwater's people had referred him to the FBI. Rick made a number of serious allegations of civil rights violations by the Lancaster Police Department against him, beginning with his arrest in on involuntary deviate sexual intercourse charges in 1975. He told the interviewing agent that:

> At approximately 3 p.m, (the day of his arrest) he was taken into an exhibits room where, on a table, appeared knives, brass knuckles, and other weapons. Officer Crump folded his arms and faced a corner, while Officer Snyder shook his fist at Haefner and said that it had been necessary for him to threaten the parents of the boys in question with Haefner's arrest or otherwise they would have killed Haefner.

Snyder said to Haefner that he knew Haefner was guilty. To this, Haefner inquired what he was being charged with. Snyder said "I'm going to charge you with something, but I don't know what the something will be." Snyder said that if the child had been his he would beat the living "shit" out of Haefner. He also told Haefner that he could get hurt in the room where he stood. Haefner said he took this as a bodily threat.

There were other charges leveled against the Lancaster Police by Haefner, including that they did not read him his rights and that he was not allowed a phone call when he was imprisoned. While they took his statement, the FBI ultimately found no evidence of a civil rights violation, and broke off contact with Rick, who continued to harangue them with letters asking when he would receive word from them. An internal memo included with his file states that "remaining In contact with him would be counterproductive."

Whether or not Rick had molested the boys in question on the date in question in the 1975 incident, there was certainly truth to the fact that Rick was, in fact, a child molester. Another former rock shop employee recalled being propositioned by Rick in 1970 at the rock shop. Rick always offered the same modus operandi for his advances. He would have the boy alone, working in the shop, and would offer him a back rub.

This boy, who knew Rick's reputation, declined. Rick finally produced a glass milk jug and said "Look, you're working so hard. Why don't you sit down with me, and we'll jerk off into this milk jug together." The boy recoiled from the prospect, telling Rick that he would "hit him with a rock hammer" if he continued to press the issue. Rick backed down that day, but would make advances on other occasions.

The boy also recalled going on field trips with Rick. The field trips were fun, and they were part of the attraction of working for Rick, along with the $1.75 per hour salary, which was high for a young man in the 1970s. On one occasion, Rick brought a six-year-old boy along, and the fifteen-year-old boy who had threatened to "hit him with a rock hammer" accompanied them. The fifteen year old slept with his rock hammer that night, but he remembered Rick inviting the blonde six-year-old into his bed.

Giggles and repeated reassurances from Rick that "it's okay, it's okay," turned into crying and screaming from the boy, at which point the fifteen year old stood up and said "Enough." Telling Rick that he would no longer help him with his projects or continue to work for him if he continued attempting to molest the six year old while he was present, the fifteen year old boy finally ended Rick's pedophilic behavior, at least while he was around.

After the molestation trial and subsequent events, Rick became increasingly isolated and paranoid. With no real friends to turn to and no prospects, Rick would occasionally return to Penn State to rant to his friend Lauren Wright about his circumstances. At one point, Rick threatened Wright's life, because he felt that someone at the college was "spreading lies" about him, just as the curators of the LA Museum had. For reasons unknown, Wright continued to entertain Rick as a friend and colleague, keeping in touch with him even after this event.

Around 1981 or 1982, one of Rick's former female classmates met with Lauren Wright and told him about her suspicions about Rick's involvement in the Aardsma murder. She recalled that Wright "said nothing, just went completely white." Apparently, Wright was surprised and disconcerted that someone else had thought the same things about Rick that he had. She also related that she had seen the newspaper coverage of the Aardsma murder in 2008 while visiting a friend in the Pennsylvania area, and had called the State Police at that time, leaving a message that suggested that they look into Rick Haefner. No one ever called her back.

There were others in the department who believed that Rick had been involved in the murder of Betsy Aardsma. "He killed that girl, plain and simple," said Deane Smith, another geology professor who had worked with Rick, and even let Rick stay at his house on a number of occasions while he finished his thesis work in the early 1970s. Smith, a microcollector, who specialized in collecting microscopic mineral samples, as well as a collector of radioactive minerals, would later die of breast cancer.

When his home in State College was cleaned out after his death, a Geiger counter was brought in to help determine which minerals were potentially radioactive and should be handled with extra care. The counter pegged at maximum, and Smith's friends thought it was

192

broken – until they walked 20 yards up the street and the levels returned to normal.

Other rumors circulated about a violent encounter Rick had been involved in during a geology class field trip. He had stayed out late the last night of the trip, and the students were loading the vans preparing to leave the following morning when Rick showed up, bruised and bloody. When asked what had happened, Rick replied that he had beaten up a woman. The decision was made to finish loading the vans and leave town without waiting for police or other unwanted attention. The specifics of this event are long forgotten, and the department was successful in burying whatever had happened that night.

One professor I spoke to even offered dim recollections of a rumor that had circulated the department around the time of the murder – a rumor that Rick had been seen leaving the library that day. Although he couldn't remember the exact source of it, he was fairly certain of the memory, and the implications that came along with it. He had not thought about it in over forty years until I spoke with him.

It was becoming more and more clear that a serious disconnect existed between what his colleagues and classmates knew and felt about him, and what they had actually done about it. Nine out of ten people who remembered Rick Haefner would inevitably either relate a strange story, or their own suspicion that he had killed Aardsma, but only Wright and Hosler had actually taken that information to someone higher up, and even then, had not bothered to make sure that it got to the police.

Somehow fear, apathy, or misplaced respect for Haefner prevented his name being given to police on a number of occasions. Meanwhile as time passed, Rick would become more and more brazen, and his crimes became more frequent and violent.

Richard Haefner, 1986-1997

If nothing else, Richard Haefner was a businessman. He had proven that with his successful rock box business. With no one to help him since the death of his father, and presumably no desire to go through another messy legal battle if he began hiring neighborhood boys again, Rick needed a new moneymaking operation. Since the molestation debacle and his reputation among the professional community had left him essentially unemployable in a museum or educational setting, he decided to start a gem show business.

The model was simple, and the money ripe for the taking. Haefner's Lost Dutchman Gembors, the business name for the company that he formed to operate the Lost Dutchman Gemboree, would contract with local meeting halls to provide vendor space. Haefner would sell the vendor space to gem sellers all across the East Coast, who would arrive to hawk their wares to the public, who paid admission. Haefner cashed in on the rental of the spaces as well as the admission fees, and a former assistant manager of the

195

show recalled that it was nothing for him to take in $30,000-$40,000 annually for a one week show in August, which required about two weeks worth of actual work to operate.

The Gemboree would also offer tours to quarries and rock hunting sites that Rick had affiliations with because of his Ph.D. In the 1980s and 1990s, many local quarries had begun to close off their operations to the public because of liability and safety concerns. Haefner, as a genuine Ph.D. in Geology with a silver tongue, was able to convince many of the quarry owners to allow him access, both for himself, and for his guided bus tours. The concept was a success, and the Gemboree outgrew its original location in Strasburg, moving to Solanco and finally Lebanon during its ten-year run. Even his brother George would occasionally come out to visit and help him set up tables at the show.

One vendor provided the following information about what a typical Lost Dutchman Gemboree looked like:

Haefner had an old blind cocker spaniel which he took everywhere. I have remembrance of a being a vendor at a gem show c. 1995 in Allentown

196

where the dog was allowed to roam around the ballroom prior to the show. It was in and out of everyone's booth. Vendors seemed anxious to remove the dog for obvious reasons without garnering the attention of Haefner. He liked confrontation, which went from civil to violent within seconds. Ten minutes prior to show time, the dog sniffs its way to the front double doors and promptly took a dump beside someone's booth. In hindsight, it was certainly an omen of things to come. He had a mentally challenged adult male, his ~15 years his junior, wearing a sheriff's star, acting as his show security. Haefner always had a screen set up at the back of the show hall at all of his shows and would invite the children to come behind the screen to learn about rocks and minerals.

The inclusion of the screen at the back of the show area is perhaps the most disturbing tidbit of all – perhaps he was still playing the role of teacher and mentor that had gotten him removed from the North Museum thirty years before.

* * *

Although Haefner played the doting son to his ailing mother Ere during the years after his father's death, he was far too busy to take care of her in any real capacity. He often left her alone, leaving her suffering from emphysema, the final effects of her chain-smoking habit that Rick hated so much. Friends and family members ended up caring for the woman who had given Rick everything he had in life, who had flown around the country with him collecting depositions for his court cases, and who had lied to police for him, supporting him no matter what trouble he got into. When she passed away in 1991, Rick stood to inherit the house on Nevin Street, but instead renounced his inheritance rights, leaving everything to his brother George, who allowed him to live in the house.

Most of Rick's assets were in other people's names, throughout his life. This seems to stem from his frequent and flagrant legal problems, and from his desire to be able to file defenses to them in forma pauperis, a legal term that literally means "in the form of a pauper." By claiming to be poor, Rick could avoid fines and restitution for his actions. George, who cared little for his brother's affairs, merely managed his inheritance, and had a willing tenant in the old family home that he now owned, three thousand miles from his life in California.

* * *

After the death of his mother, Rick's behavior was no longer subject to maternal scrutiny, and became much more scatterbrained and dangerous. He began associating with a single mother from Columbia, PA who had a 13-year old son, who would later steal from him, causing him to become involved in lawsuits against the police who didn't return the money that they recovered from the boy immediately. At one point, Rick took the boy on an unscheduled trip to Chincoteague, Virginia, where he was arrested for interfering with the custody of a minor. He was able to smooth things over with the boy's mother and beat the charges – but again, he would sue the Chincoteague Police Department for troubling him. After the woman died, Rick continued to take the boy under his wing as a sort of father figure, traveling with him and putting up with his own frequent legal troubles.

The yard at Nevin Street soon became a nuisance and an eyesore. Rick had large wooden crates and 55-gallon drums of various rocks that he would break and sell at gem shows. These crates were often covered with unsightly tarps, and there was usually other assorted junk strewn across the yard. Rick was often called into the District Court as a result of neighbors who had complained, and he was frequently cited for the poor condition of the house and yard.

Neighbors recalled Rick's unusual and combative nature, usually centered around incidents involving his dog Dudley, who Rick left to roam without a leash. Once, a neighbor observed Dudley defecating in his yard. As he was leaving in his car, he stopped and asked Rick to clean up the mess. Rick picked up the dog shit with his bare hands and threw it into the open window of the man's vehicle.

Another neighbor, who had testified against Rick in a District Court case regarding Dudley's behavior, looked out his window one night to see Rick mumbling to Dudley as they trampled the flower bed in front of his house, after which Rick bent down and punctured the tire of his car. Rick would be arrested for this.

Despite his substantial cash income from the Gemboree and his other pursuits, as well as what was left over from his successful lawsuit against Los Angeles County and the Museum of Natural History, Rick's finances deteriorated along with his other material assets after Ere's death. By 1993, he had declared bankruptcy. Since none of his assets were in his name, there was little reason to do so, except as further documentation of his financial status in case of legal troubles. Except for his substantial dealings in cash, Rick was entirely supported by his brother George's generosity and stable lifestyle.

In October of 1994, George came out from California to visit Rick, and while they were on the front porch at 217 Nevin Street, George collapsed. Rick called 911, but when the paramedics arrived, George had been moved upstairs and was resisting treatment, barricading himself into an upstairs room and attacking the paramedic team with cans of mace. When police arrived, Rick scuffled with them physically on the front porch, kicking and punching them until he could be restrained. Later explaining his actions, Rick would say "George has a fear of police officers, and I didn't want to upset him." The 200 Block of Nevin Street was sealed off for two hours, and a SERT team was called, but later released.

George was hospitalized after being arrested and given $25,000 bail. Rick was also hospitalized with heart troubles and was arrested and assigned $10,000 bail. Later, when the case goes to court, Rick pleads guilty and receives lesser charges, but not before filing an *in forma pauperis* brief listing his last employment date as 1975, with no assets, and thousands of dollars in monthly expenses. Haefner also successfully fought to avoid a psychological evaluation requested by the court after this arrest.

Whatever the truth behind Rick's finances and his bizarre behavior, the days of the Lost Dutchman Gemboree, his cash cow for the last ten years, would be numbered. The last Dutchman show would be held in August of 1996. Shortly before the show opened, someone or several individuals pried open a window at the Lebanon Expo center with a screwdriver and entered the show hall.

Police would later say that whoever did it "knew exactly what he was looking for and which booths to find it in, and took only the most valuable items" and left everything of lesser value alone. The gems were never recovered and the crime was never solved. Since gem show items are not marked or serialized, and are merely raw mineral samples that have been collected, it would have been easy for the thief to sell these at other gem and mineral shows later on.

The former head of the Lebanon Expo Center offered several recollections about the day that the Gemboree was robbed:

> "For whatever reason (Cost Savings?) Richard had hired his own overnight security people from New York instead of hiring our local Overnight Security people who were 100% honest and trustworthy.
>
> What struck me was when I arrived the morning after the overnight heist, I recall George had assisted me in opening the facility, Richard was nowhere to be found. When the Expo section was opened and the Vendors were allowed to enter.... A few vendors saw their gem cases were empty.
>
> The police were called and I tried numerous ways to contact Richard.

203

When he finally arrived in a car with
his 'overnight security' I told him of the Theft
and how/if/whether the Expo would be affected.

He walked to the section to meet with the
distraught vendors. Later he came to my office
and showed me the 'Vendor Contract' he had
with the vendors and pointed to a Clause that
read "Gem Show is not responsible for any theft
or loss"...... and he said this in such a
convincing way that either:

He was cleverly in on the heist............   Or so
dumb in efforts to Save Money that he
had ineffective security. Either way the gems
were gone."

Haefner would attempt one final Gemboree the
following year. Unable to get security or insurance for
the show after the monumental theft at the 1996 event,
he continued to collect deposits and payment for vendor
spaces anyway, even hitting the phones to attempt to
pull in as many deposits as he could, according to one
vendor:

In August of 1997, I was selling at the Marty Zinn show the weekend prior to the Lebanon show. I got a call from Haefner a couple of days prior to the show asking for the remainder of my show deposit. He was evidently calling his entire dealer pool looking for as much money as he could acquire.

When the vendors arrived the day of the show, they found that the show had been cancelled, and when they tried to receive refunds, Haefner refused to answer their calls and requests. Later, the vendors found that Haefner had never had a valid contract with the Expo Center at all for the 1997 show. This prompted another flurry of lawsuits, despite which most of the vendors never received a refund for their payments towards the aborted 1997 Lost Dutchman Gemboree.

There was one bright spot during this time. A local man, interested in gems and minerals and who had attended the Dutchman shows during their heyday, had befriended Rick and was attempting to help him turn his life around. His memories of Rick are of a disorganized yet intelligent man whose house had become a virtual rat's nest, with pathways leading from room to room as the only way to avoid the junk packed inside. He helped Rick clean, helped him tidy up the backyard to avoid fines from the city, and accompanied him on many of the Gemboree tours and to the gem shows in Tucson, where he once heard someone scream "Pedophile!" as he and Rick were leaving the venue.

Claiming that he had never seen any evidence of Rick's homosexuality, and that Rick behaved "like one of the guys, even telling gay jokes," he was nevertheless disturbed by his friend's reputation. Rick loved rocks and minerals, though, and his encyclopedic knowledge allowed his new friend to learn much, as well as to assemble a fine collection of specimens through Rick's access to quarries and rock hunting sites throughout the area. It was a beneficial friendship for both, and the man came to see a gentler side to Rick that many people never experienced:

> "Rick was very concerned with animals, and once we stopped an entire trip to the beach that we were on just to turn around to take a wounded seagull that Rick found in the road to the vet. Another time, I came over to find him feeding a mouse that lived in his home by hand,

206

and he once overturned his boat and trailer when he swerved to avoid hitting an animal in the road. In retrospect, I have to wonder if Rick was trying to atone for something."

Nevertheless, Rick's angry and vindictive nature were ever-present, and could change at the drop of a hat. Rick and his friend were kicked out of a Wendy's Restaurant on one occasion, when Rick had gotten into a verbal argument with the manager, who would not give him a cup of ice water for Dudley, the Cocker Spaniel. In court cases, Rick was a terror, eventually being banned from the local courthouse and several legal offices unless he provided prior notification that he was coming. One court docket sheet from a 1996 hearing states the following:

"Judicata Bar had been established. Plaintiff (Haefner) was given a chance to respond to defendant's motion. During his response he stood up, became extremely loud and began using profanity. The chairman intervened and advised plaintiff that this conduct was unacceptable and invited plaintiff to resume his

seat and continue his argument. Plaintiff briefly complied, but again stood up and became even more loud and abusive. He advised the panel that he believed judgment would be entered against him by this "kangaroo court" and said that he was leaving. The chairman advised plaintiff that if he left the arbitration room the panel would consider that he abandoned his right to conclude his argument and present any testimony, whereupon plaintiff left the room yelling at opposing counsel and the panel."

His long-troubling mental issues and anger management problems were coming to a head as he aged, turning him into a feared, even hated member of the community – one who no one wanted to be associated with, and who no one dared cross. Even his friend quoted earlier asked that his name not be mentioned here, because he did not want to risk reprisal or be associated with Haefner now that he was gone.

With the loss of his gem show business and the fact that none of his surviving family remained in the local area, Rick would have less and less contact with other people in the years following the failure of the Lost

Dutchman Gemboree, as well as having less and less reason to stay in the Lancaster area during his free time. Rick began making plans to do what he had wanted to do ever since the days he had studied under Lauren Wright – to move to Shoshone and live in the "Valley of Death."

Richard Haefner, 1998-2002

The last years of Richard Haefner's life were filled with the type of bizarre behavior and stumbling towards redemption that had become a hallmark of his life. By 1998, Haefner maintained an address in Shoshone, California, at Tecopa Hot Springs Road. The Tecopa Hot Springs are a series of natural mineral hot springs that bubble up through the ground in the deserts outside of Death Valley. The mineral springs are well known as a therapeutic area, and they attract a sizeable number of individuals who come to camp and bathe there.

Rick would return to Nevin Street whenever he had work to do there, or wanted to get away from the heat of the desert and his trailer home in Shoshone. In the spring, he still attended the Tucson Gem and Mineral Show in Arizona, where he would teach classes on gem cutting, being a Fellow of the Gemological Society of America. Until late 1997, he had been working on some mining sites that he had registered in the desert with the Bureau of Land Management. Rick was "mining" a thinly bedded volcanic mineral that he could then dye and sell at gem shows to make extra money.

While back east, Rick would often tow his boat down to visit a friend of his, Shirley Harding, in Chincoteague. Shirley was reluctant to discuss Rick over the phone, remarking that they were friends, and that he would often come down to visit her, bringing a bottle of wine and his small boat, and the two would go boating together. She remembered the young man Haefner had taken under his wing, who ran up a large international long distance phone bill on her home phone while he was with Rick on one trip. She did say that she and Rick "never had a romantic or sexual relationship," and had merely been friends.

On one of his trips down to visit Shirley, on January 6th, 1998, Rick decided to stop for a bottle of wine at a Liquor World liquor store at the Milltown Shopping Center in Delaware. When he arrived, he left his blind dog Dudley in the shopping cart outside the store, where two women who were leaving noticed the dog and began to discuss among themselves about whether or not they should take the dog to animal control, because it did not have tags or other identification and appeared to be abandoned by its owner.

While they were examining the dog in the cart, Rick came out of the liquor store. "What are you doing with my dog?" He asked angrily. "That's your dog? Why did you leave him alone outside?" Rick spat back a rude answer, to which the woman replied: "Some people shouldn't be allowed to have dogs." Rick returned with "Some people shouldn't be allowed to have kids."

According to the court transcripts, Catherine Schuyler, the woman who had originally seen the dog, left the sidewalk to head back to her vehicle. Rick followed her, smashing a bottle of alcohol on the side of her car. Numerous witnesses confirmed her story. When she asked him to move away from her car, Rick complied, but as she was leaving the parking lot, she stopped to write down his license plate number. It was a costly mistake. Rick walked over to the door of her car, grabbed her by the neck, and pulled her out through the window of her car, proceeding to beat her severely. Three witnesses saw Haefner kick and punch Schuyler, finally leaving, at which point she called 911. Her injuries, which included a dislocated jaw, loosened teeth, and numerous bruises and contusions, resulted in the need for $37,920 dollars in restorative dental work.

Haefner pulled his usual tricks, filing an in forma pauperis brief asking to be considered financially insolvent, representing himself, and filing countercharges against Schuyler that alleged that everything he had done to her, was actually what she had done to him. The court didn't buy it, and he was ordered to pay back $100 per month until he had fully covered the $3,504 in out of pocket costs incurred by Schuyler as a result of his brutal beating.

Oddly, despite his prior record in Pennsylvania, Haefner received a light sentence. One year in prison, of which he only needed to serve thirty days, and one year of Level II probation; completion of an anger management class and "continuation of treatment for his mental health problems," as well as the aforementioned $100 per month in restitution to the victim. Rick was able to go on about his daily llfe again, and he immediately headed off to the 1998 Tucson Gem and Mineral Show that February.

It was at Tucson in February, 1998 – fresh off his arrest in the Delaware beating -- that Rick would get into another violent fight with a woman. One of the vendors at the show told the story in an email to me:

> In 1998, we were both in Tucson for the February gem show. He was approached by a Brazilian dealer that was shorted out of his show deposits in 1997. As the dealer told me, Rick happened into the hotel room from which he was selling. The dealer asked where his money was, and within seconds, a fight ensued. Haefner grabbed the dealer's female business partner by the arm and started flipping tables full of valuable gems and mineral specimens. Two police officers appeared and joined the fray. Haefner fought with them, stomping one on the foot. Haefner was apprehended, but not after one of the police tackled him burying his face in a tough crate of rocks.

This arrest, too, would lead to nothing – the case was dismissed without prejudice three months after the attack, when the victim failed to show up in court, no doubt because she had other gem shows to attend. Haefner's luck held, this time.

Other legal problems would entangle Haefner in the fall of 1999, when his 1989 Dodge Colt, a vehicle he had purchased from a friend at Tucson and which he had outfitted as an off-road, rock-hunting car, was towed from the student parking lot at the University of Nevada, Las Vegas. Rick had a parking permit, but he alleged that he was being targeted by the University security. Fighting the case back and forth via mail from Pennsylvania, Rick sent scathing letters to the higher-ups at the University, in his typical indignant fashion.

He escalated the case all the way to the Nevada Supreme Court, and as part of the case he filed an in forma pauperis brief claiming his only income as SS Disability of $518/month. He also claimed to have $120 in cash, $2300 in property, and $700 worth of land in Inyo County at the time. He was unsuccessful in getting his vehicle returned to him, and it was auctioned off in January of 2000. Its last known whereabouts were in Nevada, where it was registered on a salvage title by a new owner as recently as 2006. Rick claimed to have lost valuable field work records and geology tools in the repossession and sale of his vehicle. It was a bitter loss, and once again Rick Haefner had to start from scratch.

* * *

"Well, Ray, I don't know much about his legal troubles, but I know he had some. I can tell you that he didn't die of a heart attack. He had a hole in his heart. I should have known the last few times we went hiking, looking for minerals. He just couldn't keep up. When it burst, he bled out into his lungs and died."

I was speaking to Bennie Troxel, Rick's old friend and a colleague of both Rick and Lauren Wright. An affable man who still loves geology and leading field trips involving college students and interested parties, even at the age of 90, Troxel couldn't seem to grasp my name when I told it to him over the phone. After several futile attempts to correct him kindly, I let it slide, figuring it didn't matter if he called me "Ray" or not.

Bennie Troxel had been a giant in the field of geology and petrology. He had met Lauren Wright as a newly-minted UCLA graduate in 1950, where they worked together for the California Division of Mines. When Wright moved to Penn State in 1961 to teach, Troxel remained behind, and through a sweetheart deal with the University, Wright was able to continue spending part of the year in Death Valley, where he and Troxel

216

would work together mapping the features and volcanic outcroppings of the Death Valley area. Troxel had apparently also worked as a petrologist, helping to discover oil and natural gas formations for some of the many gas companies operating in the 1960s.

During the last years of his life, Rick had used his connections to Wright and Troxel to help try to get a fresh start. Troxel encouraged Rick to work on field work and academic research, and in fact the two were working together on a presentation called "A Petrologic Paradox in Central Death Valley, California," which they were scheduled to present at the 54th Annual Meeting of the Geological Society of America on May 7th, 2002.

The resurgence of Rick's career was not to be, however. On March 19th, 2002, Rick began feeling chest pains, and was able to call for a medical helicopter evacuation to a Las Vegas hospital. The hole in his heart – the old congenital heart defect that plagued many of the males in the Haefner line, was starting to open. Once he arrived at the hospital and was under the care of the doctors and nurses there, his condition began to improve. Always impatient, Rick wanted to take a shower, and was frustrated that he was not allowed to do so. He yanked the IV tubes out of his arm and went

217

into the bathroom, where he collapsed and finally died – alone, bleeding out into his lungs, the same way Betsy Aardsma had died 33 years prior.

After Rick's death, his brother George handled his final arrangements. The body was removed from the hospital and taken to the Bunker Mortuary in downtown Las Vegas, where he was cremated. The whereabouts of Rick's ashes are unknown – likely scattered or in storage somewhere with George's heirs. In St. Anthony's Catholic Cemetery in Lancaster, less than three miles from his old home at Nevin Street, Richard Haefner has a marker in the Haefner family plot, next to his mother and father. The remains may be buried there, but surviving family members are not sure.

Many of the lawsuits that Rick had started or been involved in prior to his death would continue, some for as long as a year after he had died, before they could be resolved. Rick's home on Nevin Street, officially owned by George Haefner, since Rick had given up his right of inheritance when his mother died in 1991, sat vacant for a number of years, the back yard full of junk – wooden boxes and crates full of rocks, many covered by fading and cracking blue tarps. In 2006, the family cleaned up the house and prepared it for sale, throwing out many of Rick's personal belongings in the process.

The story behind the house, and the feelings that emanate from it, remain. One can still see the corner of the garage where Ere boxed Rick in and berated him about killing "that girl," and the bedroom on the upper floor where Rick lived out his whole life. In the gravel off the alleyway in front of the double doors where Rick's rock shop entered the street, there are still bits and pieces of exotic rocks and minerals – red granite, obsidian, and other stones that are out of place among the grey limestone gravel of Lancaster County. Those rocks, and the granite tombstone at St. Anthony's two miles away, are all that remains of Richard Haefner in Lancaster County – except, perhaps for the memories of the people he hurt, wronged, and violated.

Portrait of a Murder Suspect

After everything that has come to light about Richard Haefner, it is easy to see that he could have, and most likely did, murder Betsy Aardsma that day in the Penn State Pattee Library. But why did he do it, and what else about him makes him such a compelling suspect in her murder? There are a number of different aspects of Haefner's personality, but before going into the forensic psychology of Richard Haefner, it might help to understand possible scenarios.

Rick could easily have fit into the homosexual scenario, especially with his penchant for bringing younger boys up to the core. Although there would be no explanation for where the boy would have went during this, if there were indeed two men, an older male companion could have fled out one side of the core, or even have waited around to join the gathering crowd of spectators after Haefner fled. This theory is possible, but not entirely plausible. It hinges on the idea that Rick may have felt that Betsy had observed him, when in reality she had not, and he decided to do something about it. It also does not explain why his partner would not have ever gone to the State Police with the story, even anonymously.

The most likely scenario is that Rick's rage and obsession with Betsy grew stronger after she broke up with him. Much as can be seen in the Mary Kelling story, Rick had a tendency to fixate on people and build up a false sense of his relationship with them. He may have been hurt by the rejection Betsy gave him, and probably brooded about it before deciding that he would go and convince her otherwise. Since he stayed up at Penn State over the Thanksgiving holiday, he may have anticipated running into her, thinking that it would be a happy event, that she would be excited to see him. He could easily have followed her from Atherton or observed her returning the night before the murder.

We also do not know about the full extent of his relationship with Aardsma, or when they did break up. It's obvious that they had talked, because he knew things about her that no one else knew. But the timeline provided for the events is all Rick's, and it serves to make Rick look innocent. He claimed that they broke up at the end of October, a month before the murders. What if they had not? She may have broken up with him a week before, or may even have finally told him off that day in the core, when he ran into her. All Betsy's roommate could remember was that Rick had come around a few times.

"The fact that he remembered specific dates, would have been a red flag to me," said Detective Jan Walters, now retired after years of service in the Lancaster City Police and the Lancaster District Attorney's Office. Most individuals who are being honest in a polygraph test are vague about dates – "It happened late last month," as opposed to "It happened at 2:00 PM on October 29th." Rick's recollections of specific dates indicate that he came prepared to the State Police interview.

Whether or not his stories of their relationship are truthful, there are certainly reasons that Rick might have killed her. Rick may have felt threatened by Betsy's reaction, if indeed he tried to "get her back." If she had done as Mary had done – told him to leave her alone, hinted that she might tell police or someone else – Rick would have been threatened. He already had the Kelling incident in his past, as well as the North Museum problems and the beating incident on the field trip. Lauren Wright, his advisor, was aware of his past with women. How many more shenanigans could he engage in before he would be disciplined, or even asked to leave the program?

Perhaps Rick was just obsessed with her. She fit into his "type," as evidenced by Mary Kelling a year earlier. A strong, college educated woman, shorter, with brown hair, attractive and outgoing. Her interests were even the same – Africa, the Peace Corps. In Rick's mind, perhaps he simply could not deal with losing this girl, who he had mentioned to his friends and parents that he was dating. Pressure from his mother to date, to appear normal, may also have figured into his decision to visit her.

Betsy would not have been afraid to see Rick approach, and may have welcomed him as he came down the aisle to see her. Whatever the situation, no one will ever know, but it seems plausible that Rick would have been able to engage in a short conversation with her. The killing itself seems almost secondary; almost accidental – perhaps, in a moment of rage, he snapped, pulled out the knife, and killed her. Or perhaps he had carried the knife with him, open, but hidden at his side as he walked down the aisle. There were no defensive wounds on Aardsma's body – she was obviously taken by surprise.

One interesting piece of the puzzle that suggests that Haefner would have had a murder weapon handy is the commonplace nature of knives in the Geology department in the 1960s. One of the most basic tests involved in determining the makeup of a rock or mineral is a hardness test – how hard is it relative to steel? Can it be scratched by a knife or screwdriver, or is it impervious? Knives can also be used to cleave, or split, rocks along cleavage points.

A number of geology students from that time period recalled that it was normal to carry a pocketknife at all times, not just for fieldwork, but out of general habit. More so than most students, Haefner would have had every reason to carry a pocketknife because of his chosen field of study. Simply having the weapon along with him could have turned the situation deadly.

Looking at Rick's behavior in the years after the murder, it is clear that this is a man who had "a demon in him," as his cousin Chris had said. One of the tools used by modern psychologists and criminal investigators to assess an individual's level of psychopathic or antisocial mental illness is the Hare's Psychopathy Checklist, Revised or PCL-R. This is the same test that was given posthumously to the Columbine shooters, Eric

Harris and Dylan Klebold, to determine what their level of personality disorder might have been.

The PCL-R is a series of twenty questions that cover a range of behaviors and personality traits and that can be answered on a scale of 0 to 2, with zero being "does not apply," one meaning "somewhat applies," and two being "definitely applies." Individuals with no criminal record score around 5 on the test, while most career criminals and prison inmates score around 22. Clinical diagnosis of psychopathy begins at a score of 30 or more. A "perfect" score of 40 is almost unheard of.

Out of curiosity, I scored Rick's behavior on the PCL-R. I had to run the test twice, because I couldn't believe the results. The first time he scored a 32, and the second time, 34. Informal? Perhaps. Nevertheless, the results are a clear indicator of an antisocial or psychopathic personality. Rick himself admitted to courts that he suffered from depression and bipolar disorder, so it's not outside the realm of possibility that he had further mental problems. In a number of instances, he fought hard to avoid undergoing psychological evaluation in combination with his court cases.

Dr. Leonard Marlin Cohen might disagree with the assessment of Rick as a psychopath, although Hare's PCL-R wasn't available when Cohen knew Rick. A former Correctional Psychologist at Philadelphia's notorious Eastern State Penitentiary, as well as at the State Correctional Facility at Camp Hill, Cohen's resume and experience certainly qualified him to assess even the most violent felons.

As the psychiatrist who examined Rick as a part of his defense during his 1976 involuntary deviate sexual intercourse and corruption of minors, he performed an eight-hour formal examination of Haefner's psyche using objective measure tests (where he would ask questions with definite answers to demonstrate Haefner's ability to deal with anxiety), as well as projective measure tests (also known as Rorschach ink-blot tests, where the subject's own perceptions are used to describe the blots).

Cohen came to the conclusion that Haefner:

"is of superior intellectual endowments and of course, having gone ahead and earned a Bachelor's and Master's and a Doctor of Philosophy Degree as well as on Cohen's Wexler Adult Intelligent Scale, Haefner is *in a superior range...he's of the upper five percent of the general population."*

He also concluded that, when he examined Haefner, there was "nothing to suggest that he was out of touch with reality or that he was psychotic," however, "he may, on occasion, block and become confused to the extent that it is quite possible that he would say something that is absolutely not true."

More importantly, Cohen also found that, towards the end of the inkblot tests, Haefner became anxious and began to "respond with uncontrolled emotion." He concluded his diagnosis by suggesting that that "under stress, this man is going to become confused and is going to be emotionally liable." He would "become flustered, he would not be able to concentrate effectively. His attention span would fluctuate, and he would then be thinking straight."

Perhaps Haefner became confused, emotional, and uncontrolled before stabbing Aardsma, then began to think straight and walked out of the core to get help? The scenario is certainly plausible, whether or not he was a psychopath.

None of this information was available to investigators at the time of the Aardsma murder, and no one who was empowered to press the issue or investigate further into Rick's life had reason to believe that he was anything but what he appeared to be: A clean-cut, intelligent young man who was working in a field that he loved and who obviously had a certain level of respect and decorum that many college students of the era lacked.

Here was a man who was always wearing his khaki pants, sport coat, and tie with a button down shirt and neatly kept hair, in an era of hippies and drug users, tie-dye and torn jeans. Rick was a man who "dressed like a gentleman," and who "looked like a student" – and who could very realistically have panicked and walked away from a murder.

Epilogue

It is my opinion that there is something about this case that is too electric to be mentioned or cleared officially. Whether it is the fact that the Penn State University and its employees did so little to police their own ranks or to properly report the information that had been given to them in 1969, or whether it is because of some other reason, I do not know. For whatever reason, Penn State seems unwilling to own up to the facts of history – The Daily Collegian articles were recently removed by the college from the internet, and a visitor to the office was told that they are "no longer allowed to give out articles about the Aardsma murder."

From an evidentiary standpoint, it seems unfortunately rather likely that the cards the Pennsylvania State Police are holding in their file at Rockview are a bluff – and they cannot play their hand because they do not have a living suspect, a confession, or other physical evidence to back it up. My guess is that, at this point, and possibly as far back as the day of the murder, no one could have been convicted of it, based on what evidence was available. Sloppy as it was, the killer was able to commit the perfect crime.

"The problem with the Aardsma murder doesn't start with the case file. It doesn't start with the State Police, and it doesn't start with the college," says Sascha Skucek, Penn State University lecturer and writer on the Aardsma case. "The problem with the Aardsma murder starts with the witnesses." These individuals, going about their lives, engaged in normal daily activities, were presented with a series of bizarre occurrences that they could not completely process or properly recall. The result, perhaps, is that the case was unsolvable from the moment the killer walked out the front door of Pattee.

Recently, the State Police released a Vaughn Act listing of all of the information in the Aardsma file. This fifty-eight page document covers, with a brief description, everything in the file. Items are marked as "grade transcript," "letter," "physical evidence," "investigation notes," etc., and are then listed as to what part of the PA Statute prohibits their release under the Right to Know Law. Much of what is in this file seems unlikely to produce a conviction, yet the Vaughn Index ensures that it will never be released to the general public, at least until the case is archived.

As far as Richard Haefner, the Pennsylvania State Police Public Information Officer at Rockview released a statement regarding his status in the case as currently viewed by the police:

As you know, we do not release suspect information. Haefner's name came up, however, he is not a suspect. He a person who we believe may have possibly had more information about the crime. This is still an active investigation and there are several individuals that we are attempting to develop.

The retired officers who worked the case for years are less circumspect, thought. "This is the best thing I've heard about this case in 41 years," said Mike Mutch, who discovered the semen in the Core the night of Betsy's murder. "I think you've got your man," said Ron Tyger, another original officer on the case. "No reason to keep beating the bushes." Corporal Roger Smith, who left the case in 2005, said only that "Haefner's certainly a strong suspect," when asked in fall 2010. George Keibler, who originally did not recall Haefner when presented with the name in 2008, said in

2009 that "I remember the name, but I don't recall him being considered as a suspect [at the time]."

Time -- for so long the bane of investigators in the Aardsma murder -- is still working against everyone. The witnesses, friends, and many of the individuals investigated by police in 1969 are dead, as is Haefner, the suspect, and along with him Uafinda, Erdley, Allen, Bland, Lisle, Spencer, Meserole, Rose...The list goes on and on. Each passing day, the case becomes less and less likely to be solved.

At seventy-five years after the date of the crime, the case will legally be transferred to the State Police Records repository in Harrisburg, at which time it may be possible to legally compel the State Police to release some of the information in the files via the Pennsylvania Right to Know Law. Of course, this is still almost forty years away from happening, so it doesn't even merit discussion.

The murder weapon remains a mystery. Neither of the two knives recovered by the Police has ever been publicly acknowledged to be the murder weapon, and one of them may even be missing. In my opinion, if Rick committed the murder, the weapon is likely long gone. It could have been thrown out the window of a car anywhere between State College and Lancaster; it could have been buried or discarded by Rick or his mother when he returned home.

It may have been unknowingly discarded by the family when the house at Nevin Street was cleaned out, or it could be at the bottom of one of the many abandoned mines and now-flooded quarries Rick loved to go rock-hunting in. In any case, it will likely never resurface.

It is my sincere hope that the vital piece of information that could solve this case will eventually come out. At this point, it would be a Pyrrhic victory for all involved. Dozens of State Troopers, college officials, and others who were involved or concerned about the outcome of this case have gone to their graves, never knowing for sure who had killed Betsy Aardsma in Pattee that day so many years ago. Even a signed confession at this point would not be able to undo all of the time spent trying to understand something that is as inscrutable as the murder of a vibrant, cheerful young college student from Holland, Michigan. What's more – nothing will bring Betsy back, or give her family the years that they have lost because of the killer's actions.

233

Further Reading

In this section, I have included a number of the sources used to write this book, as well as recent articles about the case that have come out over the past few years.

In addition to these sources, this book required dozens of interviews, via telephone, email, and in person. Many of the individuals asked not to be named. I have tried to respect their wishes as best I can, and will not cite the names of these individuals herein.

Along with these articles, literally thousands of pages of court documents and transcripts from Richard Haefner's many criminal and civil trials, as well as documents related to the police investigation of the Aardsma murder and Richard Haefner obtained through the Freedom of Information Act were consulted. There are a number of helpful documents that have been released through Pennsylvania Right to Know Law Requests as well. These documents proved to be invaluable sources for understanding the case and how it progressed.

Daily Collegian Articles:

"Cries for Help Unheeded" -- Daily Collegian, 12/2/69

"Police Continue Search" -- Daily Collegian, 12/4/69

"Coed Murder Still Unsolved" -- Daily Collegian, 1/6/70

"Police Sketch" -- Daily Collegian, 1/10/70

"Rape Cases Not Linked with Aardsma Murder Query" -- Daily Collegian, 1/20/70

"Police Visit Ann Arbor" -- Daily Collegian, 1/25/70

"State Policeman Denies Rumor of Suspect in Aardsma Murder" -- Daily Collegian, 2/12/70

"Kimmel Denies Rumors, Says Stigma Attached" -- Daily Collegian, 2/14/70

"Kimmel Says Student Chased Witness in Aardsma Murder" -- Daily Collegian, 3/5/70

"University Sets Reward For Murder Information" -- Daily Collegian, 3/31/70

"Police Probe Possible Link in Rape, Stabbing Case" -- Daily Collegian, 3/31/70

"It Happened Nine Months Ago" -- Daily Collegian, 8/27/70

"Aardsma Case Still Mystery" -- Daily Collegian, 1/15/71

"Attacker Flees Coed" -- Daily Collegian, 2/5/71

"1969 Murder Goes Unsolved" -- Daily Collegian,
5/18/81
"Murder Conjures Memories of Pattee Stabbing" -- Daily
Collegian, 3/11/87
"A Vexing Mystery." Daily Collegian, 11/12/89
"Investigation of Bundy's Link to Aardsma Murder
Inconclusive." Daily Collegian, 11/12/89

National Newspaper Articles:
"Pennsylvania Stabbing Fatal for Holland Coed" --
Holland Evening Sentinel, 11/29/69
"Student Collapses In Library" -- Holland Evening
Sentinel, Holland, MI 11/29/69
"County Coed In Library Unaware Girl Was Dead" --
Delaware County (PA) Daily Times, PA 12/1/1969
"State Police Are Hunting Two Men in Coed's Death" --
Lebanon Daily News, Lebanon, PA 12/1/1969
"State Police Probe Penn State Coed Slaying" --
Newcastle News, Newcastle, PA 12/1/1969
"Penn State Coed Had Fine Future" -- Uniontown News,
Uniontown, PA 12/1/1969
"2 Suspects Sought in Co-Ed's Death" -- Holland Evening
Sentinel, Holland, MI 12/2/69

"Search for Slayer of Girl Pushed" -- The Daily News, Huntingdon, PA 12/4/69

"Two Volunteer Data In Probe Of Slaying" -- The Daily News, Huntingdon & Mt. Union, PA 12/6/69

"No A-1 Suspects In Coed Murder" -- Holland Evening Sentinel, Holland, MI 12/13/69

"Kin of Murdered Woman Implore Courts to Spare Lives of All Killers" -- The Capital Times, Madison, WI 1/13/72

Recent Articles:

"Who Killed Betsy Aardsma?" State College Magazine, 1999

"The Last Reason." State College Magazine, 4/04

"Web Site devoted to Cold Case." Holland Sentinel, March, 2008

"Murder in the Stacks." Philadelphia Inquirer, 7/31/08

"They Are Old Men Now." Harrisburg Patriot News, 12/7/08

"Decades Later, Penn State Library Slaying Unsolved." Chicago Tribune, 8/2/08

"Murder in the Core." State College Magazine, January 2009.

"Who Killed Betsy Aardsma?" The Penn Stater, Sept./Oct. 2009

"Mystery of the Girl in the Stacks Continues to Intrigue Public." Pittsburgh Post-Gazette, 10/25/09

"Unsolved 1969 Murder Haunts Penn State Pittsburgh Tribune-Review, 11/28/09

"Case Closed?" State College Magazine, 10/10

"Who Killed Betsy Aardsma?" Lancaster Sunday News, 10/10/10

"The Real Life Cold Case of Betsy Aardsma" Examiner.com, 10/14/10

Centre Daily Times Blog CDT Online, 10/22/10.

Interview with Todd Matthews of NAMUS/Missing Pieces Radio Show Web-only, 11/15/10

Contact Information

If you wish to contact me, whether to order copies of the book, to discuss the case or any questions you might have, or to provide information regarding the case, you can do so by emailing me: info@whokilledbetsy.org. Some of the best information I have received to date has come from individuals who heard about this case and chose to break their silence to speak to me.

38592493R00139

Made in the USA
Lexington, KY
15 January 2015